Sushi

Cookbook for Beginners

Easy & Delicious Sushi Recipes Dive You into the World of Sushi
Making | Rich Fusion of Asian Flavors and Artistic Presentation

Dorothy Carpenter

Table of Contents

Introduction

Welcome to the amazing world of sushi, where innovation meets culture on a beautiful plate. In this cookbook, you will dive into the exciting world of sushi, learning its rich history and origin, the art of sushi-making, staple ingredients, and techniques. Let this book be your passport to the intricate universe of sushi, providing you with everything you need to savor this delicacy. Sushi, with its rich fusion of flavors and artistic presentation, has captivated food aficionados across the globe, captivating their hearts and tantalizing their taste buds with every exquisite bite.

At its core, sushi is the perfect way to enhance the beauty of fresh ingredients. Each component of the sushi, from the richness of fish to the simplicity of rice, each simple yet beautiful component comes together to create the perfect bite.

So, join us as we dive into the world of sushi, where every roll tells a story and every bite is a celebration of flavor and tradition. Let's roll!

The Art of Sushi Making

Sushi is considered as a culinary icon worldwide. It is considered as a testament to the essence of the rich flavors and artistic techniques of the Japanese cuisine. Originating from Japan centuries ago, it has transformed from a local staple food to a prized delicacy everywhere.

History of Sushi

The origins of sushi trace back to ancient Japan, where it began as a simple method of preserving fish. Early techniques involved fermenting fish with rice and salt, a process that not only preserved the fish but also imparted a unique flavor. Over time, sushi evolved, with different regions of Japan developing their own styles and variations. One of the earliest forms of sushi, known as Narezushi, dates back to the 3rd century AD. In this method, fish was salted and fermented with rice for several months, resulting in a pungent yet flavorful dish. Over the centuries, sushi continued to evolve, eventually giving rise to Edomae sushi during the Edo period (17th-19th centuries). Edomae sushi, named after the bustling fish markets of Edo (now Tokyo), featured fresh fish served atop vinegared rice, a stark departure from the fermented sushi of earlier times.

While sushi had long been cherished in Japan, its introduction to the world came much later. In the mid-20th century, Japanese immigrants brought sushi to the United States, where it initially gained popularity among adventurous diners. Over time, sushi bars began to proliferate in cities like Los Angeles and New York, introducing a wider audience to the delights of sushi. Today, sushi can be found in virtually every corner of the globe, from traditional sushiya in Japan to trendy fusion restaurants worldwide. Yet, no matter where it's enjoyed, the essence of sushi remains the same – a celebration of tradition, craftsmanship, and the simple pleasure of good food.

Common Types of Sushi

Sushi comes in many different shapes, flavors and sizes, each with its own specific and unique style. some of the common types of sushi are

Nigiri

Nigiri sushi exemplifies simplicity and elegance. A small mound of vinegared rice, seasoned just right, is topped with a slice of fresh, raw fish. The rice is gently formed by skilled hands to provide the perfect base for the fish, ensuring that each bite harmonizes the flavors of the rice and the fish. Common types of fish used for nigiri include maguro (tuna), sake (salmon), hamachi (yellowtail), and ebi (shrimp). Sometimes, a dab of wasabi is placed between the fish and the rice for an extra kick.

Maki

Maki sushi offers endless possibilities for creativity and flavor combinations. The process starts with a sheet of nori spread over a bamboo mat, then a layer of seasoned rice is evenly spread over the nori. Fillings such as fish, vegetables, and sauces are arranged in a line along the center of the rice. Using the bamboo mat, the sushi is carefully rolled into a cylinder and sliced into bite-sized pieces. Varieties range from the simple cucumber or avocado roll to more elaborate creations like the spider roll, filled with soft-shell crab, avocado, and cucumber.

Sashimi

Sashimi is the purest form of sushi, showcasing the quality and freshness of the fish. Thin slices of raw fish, typically served without rice, are arranged artfully on a plate. The fish is often accompanied by garnishes such as shredded daikon radish, shiso leaves, and pickled ginger. Popular choices for sashimi include maguro (tuna), sake (salmon), hamachi (yellowtail), and tako (octopus). The delicate slices of fish melt in your mouth, offering a taste experience like no other.

Tempura Roll

Tempura rolls combine the crunchiness of tempura-fried ingredients with the familiar flavors of sushi. Tempura shrimp, vegetables, or even soft-shell crab are dipped in a light batter and deep-fried until golden and crispy. These fried delicacies are then rolled with rice and nori, creating a delightful contrast of textures. Tempura rolls are often served with a dipping sauce, such as soy sauce mixed with grated daikon radish or a tangy tempura dipping sauce (tentsuyu).

Rainbow Roll

The rainbow roll is as visually stunning as it is delicious. This vibrant creation features a California roll (crab, avocado, and cucumber) topped with an assortment of thinly sliced fish, arranged in a colorful rainbow pattern. The combination of flavors and textures—creamy avocado, tender crab, and fresh fish—makes each bite a burst of delight. A drizzle of sweet eel sauce or spicy mayo adds the perfect finishing touch.

Unagi (Eel) Nigiri

Unagi nigiri is a beloved sushi delicacy that showcases the rich, savory flavor of grilled freshwater eel. The eel is marinated in a sweet and savory sauce, then grilled to perfection, resulting in tender, caramelized slices of eel. Each slice is carefully placed atop a small mound of rice and brushed with more of the luscious sauce, creating a harmonious blend of flavors.

Tamago (Egg) Nigiri

Tamago nigiri is a sweet and savory treat that satisfies both the palate and the soul. The tamago, or Japanese omelet, is made by whisking together eggs, sugar, and sometimes dashi (fish stock), then cooking the mixture in thin layers until it forms a light, fluffy omelet. The finished omelet is sliced into rectangles and placed atop bite-sized portions of rice. The sweet, custard-like texture of the tamago pairs beautifully with the vinegary rice, creating a delightful contrast of flavors.

Hand Rolls (Temaki)

Hand rolls, or temaki, are perfect for those who prefer their sushi fresh and customizable. A sheet of nori is filled with rice, fish, vegetables, and sauces, then rolled into a cone shape by hand. The open end of the cone allows for easy eating, making hand rolls a popular choice for sushi lovers on the go. Fillings can vary widely, from spicy tuna and cucumber to crab salad and avocado, giving diners endless options to suit their tastes.

Selection of Sushi Ingredients

When selecting ingredients for sushi, it's crucial to prioritize freshness, quality, and flavor balance to ensure an authentic and enjoyable dining experience.

Rice

Sushi rice, or "shari," serves as the cornerstone of sushi, providing a delicate texture and subtly sweet flavor that complements the other ingredients. When choosing rice for sushi, meticulous attention to detail is essential
Opt for short-grain Japanese rice varieties like Koshihikari, Tamaki Gold, or Calrose, prized for their stickiness and ability to hold together in sushi rolls.
Look for rice specifically labeled as sushi rice, indicating that it has been polished to the ideal degree and possesses the appropriate moisture content.
Examine the rice grains for uniformity in size and shape, ensuring even cooking and consistent texture.
Assess the freshness of the rice by checking for plump, intact grains free from any signs of moisture or mold.
Consider the cooking process; sushi rice should be

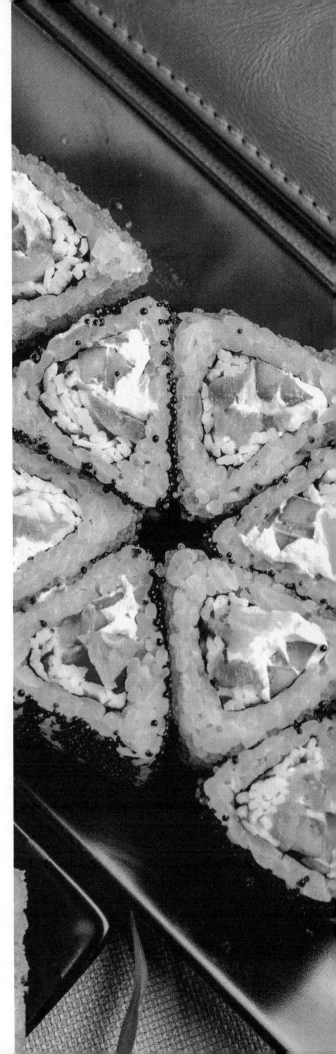

cooked with the right balance of water to achieve a firm yet tender consistency, with each grain distinct and slightly sticky when pressed together.

Fish

Fresh, high-quality fish is paramount in sushi, dictating the dish's taste, texture, and safety. When selecting fish for sushi, several factors come into play:

Prioritize sushi-grade fish, meticulously handled and stored to minimize the risk of foodborne illness.

Look for fish with clear, bright eyes and vibrant, metallic skin, indicative of freshness and optimal flavor.

Take into account the seasonality of fish; certain species are at their peak freshness during specific times of the year.

Assess the fish's aroma; it should exude a clean, ocean-like scent, devoid of any overpowering fishiness.

Gauge the texture of the fish; it should feel firm and resilient to the touch, bouncing back when pressed, signaling freshness and quality.

Nori (Seaweed)

Nori, or dried seaweed sheets, serves as the wrapper for many sushi rolls, imparting a distinct umami flavor and satisfying crunch. When selecting nori, meticulous attention to detail ensures the best results:

Choose nori sheets that boast a deep, dark green hue and uniform texture, signaling quality and freshness.

Prioritize nori that is crisp and dry, with minimal moisture content to prevent sogginess when used in sushi rolls.

Consider the thickness of the nori sheets; thinner varieties are easier to roll and offer a delicate texture, while thicker sheets provide a more robust flavor profile.

Inspect the nori for any signs of damage or tears, as these imperfections can compromise the integrity of the sushi roll.

Vegetables

Vegetables play a pivotal role in sushi, contributing freshness, texture, and vibrant flavors to each bite. When selecting vegetables for sushi, attention to freshness and quality is paramount:

Choose fresh, crisp vegetables that are in season for optimal flavor and texture.

Look for vegetables with vibrant colors and firm textures, indicating freshness and superior quality.

Use a variety of vegetables, including cucumber, avocado, carrots, radishes, and sprouts, to add complexity and visual appeal to sushi rolls.

Ensure thorough washing and preparation of vegetables to remove any dirt or debris, enhancing food safety and cleanliness.

Condiments and Garnishes

Condiments and garnishes elevate the flavor profile and

presentation of sushi, offering an array of tastes and textures to tantalize the palate. When selecting condiments and garnishes, thoughtful consideration ensures harmonious combinations:

Choose premium-quality soy sauce, preferably Japanese soy sauce, for dipping sushi rolls and sashimi, with options ranging from light to dark and low-sodium varieties.

Select fresh wasabi, either in paste or powder form, for a pungent kick and distinctive flavor that complements the sushi's delicate taste.

Explore additional garnishes such as pickled ginger (gari), sesame seeds, scallions, and micro greens to add texture, acidity, and visual appeal to sushi dishes.

Experiment with different condiments and garnishes to find complementary pairings that enhance the flavors of the sushi ingredients while delighting the senses.

Essential Tools for Making Sushi

Achieving perfect sushi requires not only skill but also the right tools. From precise slicing to expert rolling, each tool plays a crucial role in crafting sushi worthy of admiration.

Sushi Knife (Yanagiba)

The sushi knife, commonly known as Yanagiba, is a specialized Japanese knife designed for slicing fish with precision. Its long, slender blade is single-edged, allowing for effortless cuts through raw fish without tearing or crushing the delicate flesh. The sharpness of the Yanagiba ensures clean, smooth slices, crucial for presenting visually appealing sashimi and neatly rolled sushi.

It is comprised of a single-edged blade which provides enhanced control and precision while cutting.

The blade is thin and sharp and allows for clean slicing, minimizing damage to ingredients.

Considered ideal for sashimi and sushi rolls. Ensures uniform slices for an aesthetically pleasing presentation.

The sushi knife is considered as a professional-grade tool. It is considered essential for achieving restaurant-quality results in sushi preparation.

Bamboo Rolling Mat (Makisu)

The bamboo rolling mat, or Makisu, is an indispensable tool for rolling sushi neatly and tightly. Consisting of thin bamboo slats woven together with cotton string, the Makisu provides the flexibility and structure required for shaping sushi rolls. It enables the even distribution of ingredients within the roll while ensuring a firm, compact shape.

It helps create tightly rolled sushi. The mat ensures that all the ingredients are firmly packed for a cohesive roll.

Easy to clean and reuse. Simply wipe clean with a damp cloth after each use.

Flexible for creating any desired shape. It allows for the formation of various sushi roll shapes and sizes.

Provides consistent results. Helps maintain the integrity and uniformity of sushi rolls for professional presentation.

Rice Paddle (Shamoji)

The rice paddle, known as Shamoji, is a flat, spatula-like utensil essential for handling and shaping sushi rice. Its broad, flat surface prevents rice from sticking, facilitating the mixing and spreading of rice during sushi preparation. The Shamoji is particularly crucial for evenly distributing seasoned rice over nori sheets when making sushi rolls.

Facilitates mixing and spreading of rice, helping with an even distribution of ingredients for consistent flavor.

Greatly prevents rice from sticking. The smooth surface prevents rice grains from clumping together.

It allows for precise rice distribution which is essential for achieving uniform layers of rice in sushi rolls.

The paddle is made of non-reactive materials. Typically crafted from wood or plastic to prevent rice from absorbing unwanted flavors.

An essential tool for sushi rice preparation as it is used for shaping and handling rice.

Sushi Mat (Hangiri)

The sushi mat, or Hangiri, is a traditional wooden tub used for mixing sushi rice with vinegar seasoning. Its flat-bottomed, round shape provides ample surface area for evenly dispersing the vinegar throughout the rice, imparting the characteristic tangy flavor essential to sushi rice. The Hangiri's wooden construction also absorbs excess moisture from the rice, helping to achieve the desired texture and consistency.

Promotes even mixing of vinegar seasoning as it ensures uniform distribution of flavor throughout the rice.

It is a traditional tool for sushi rice preparation and has been used for centuries in Japanese cuisine to achieve authentic sushi rice.

Wooden construction absorbs excess moisture, helping maintain the ideal texture and consistency of sushi rice.

Large surface area for efficient mixing. The mat greatly allows for thorough incorporation of vinegar without crushing rice grains.

Facilitates proper seasoning of rice. It is integral for achieving the signature taste and texture of sushi rice.

Rice Cooker

A rice cooker is a modern kitchen appliance indispensable for preparing sushi rice with consistent results. It

automates the cooking process, accurately controlling temperature and cooking time to achieve perfectly cooked rice every time. Sushi rice requires precise cooking to attain the ideal texture and stickiness essential for sushi preparation, making a rice cooker a valuable tool for both amateur and professional sushi chefs.

Ensures consistent rice cooking and maintains precise temperature and cooking time for optimal results.

Simplifies sushi rice preparation by automating the cooking process, saving time and effort.

Offers various settings for different rice types. It allows for customization based on rice variety and desired texture.

Keeps rice warm until ready to use. The sushi rice can be kept at an ideal serving temperature without drying out.

It saves time and effort in the kitchen. Streamlining the sushi-making process for efficient meal preparation.

How to Make Sushi

Crafting sushi is a meticulous process that revolves around precise steps and ingredient preparation. From selecting the freshest fish to mastering the art of rice cooking, every aspect of sushi making contributes to its exquisite taste and presentation.

Preparation of Basic Ingredients
Before beginning the sushi-making process, it's crucial to properly prepare the basic ingredients.

Sushi Rice
Measure out 2 cups of sushi rice and place it in a fine-mesh strainer.

Rinse the rice under cold water, gently swishing it around with your fingers until the water runs clear. This helps remove excess starch.

Transfer the rinsed rice to a pot or rice cooker and add 2 ½ cups of water.

Let the rice soak in the water for about 30 minutes to allow it to absorb moisture evenly.

Cook the rice according to the instructions of your rice cooker or bring it to a boil over medium-high heat, then reduce the heat to low and let it simmer, covered, for about 15-20 minutes until the water is absorbed and the rice is tender.

Once cooked, remove the pot from heat and let the rice sit, covered, for an additional 10 minutes to steam.

While the rice is still warm, transfer it to a large wooden or glass bowl. Drizzle sushi vinegar (a mixture of rice vinegar, sugar, and salt) over the rice and gently fold it in using a wooden spoon or spatula, being careful not to mash the grains. Continue folding until the vinegar is evenly distributed and the rice is slightly sticky and glossy.

Nori Sheets

Open the package of nori sheets just before you're ready to use them to prevent them from becoming stale.

If the nori sheets are uncut, use kitchen scissors to cut them in half crosswise, creating rectangular sheets that are easier to work with.

To toast the nori, hold each sheet with tongs and pass it over an open flame (such as a gas burner) or quickly toast it in a dry skillet over medium heat for a few seconds on each side until it becomes crisp and fragrant. Be careful not to burn the nori; it should turn a slightly darker shade of green and become brittle.

Fillings

Prepare your desired fillings based on your preferences. Common options include:

Cucumber

Peel the cucumber and cut it into thin, long strips.

Avocado

Cut the avocado in half, remove the pit, scoop out the flesh, and slice it into thin wedges.

Cooked Shrimp

Peel and devein the shrimp, then slice them in half lengthwise or leave them whole.

Crab Meat

If using imitation crab sticks, simply slice them into thin strips. For real crab meat, remove any shells and break the meat into small chunks.

Smoked Salmon

Slice the smoked salmon into thin strips or bite-sized pieces.

Arrange the prepared fillings on a plate or cutting board so they're easily accessible when assembling the sushi rolls.

Making Different Types of Sushi

Hosomaki (Thin Rolls)

Lay a nori sheet on a bamboo sushi mat.

Spread a thin layer of sushi rice evenly over the nori, leaving about ½ inch of the seaweed uncovered at the top.

Arrange your desired fillings horizontally across the middle of the rice.

Roll the sushi tightly using the bamboo mat, applying gentle pressure as you roll.

Using a sharp, wet knife, slice the roll into bite-sized pieces.

Futomaki (Thick Rolls)

Place a nori sheet on the bamboo mat, shiny side down.

Spread a slightly thicker layer of sushi rice over the nori, covering the entire sheet.

Arrange fillings in a line across the middle of the rice.

Roll the sushi tightly using the bamboo mat, ensuring the

fillings are enclosed within the rice.

Slice the roll into thick pieces using a sharp, wet knife.

Nigiri Sushi

Wet your hands with water to prevent sticking.

Grab a handful of sushi rice and shape it into a small oval or rectangular mound.

Place a thin slice of fish or cooked seafood on top of the rice mound.

Press the fish onto the rice gently with your fingers.

Serve the nigiri sushi with a small dab of wasabi between the rice and fish, if desired.

Inside-Out Rolls (Uramaki)

Place a sheet of plastic wrap on your sushi mat.

Cover the plastic wrap with a layer of sushi rice, leaving a small border at the edges.

Flip the rice-covered mat over so the rice is facing down on the plastic wrap.

Arrange fillings on the nori sheet.

Roll the sushi tightly using the bamboo mat, ensuring the rice is on the outside.

Sprinkle sesame seeds or tobiko over the exposed rice, if desired.

Slice the roll into bite-sized pieces using a sharp, wet knife.

Temaki (Hand Rolls)

Place a nori sheet on your hand or a flat surface, shiny side down, with one corner pointing towards you.

Spread a thin layer of sushi rice over the bottom half of the nori sheet.

Add fillings diagonally across the rice.

Roll the nori sheet into a cone shape, starting from the bottom corner and rolling towards the opposite corner.

Seal the hand roll by moistening the top corner of the nori with water.

Serve immediately, as hand rolls are best enjoyed fresh.

Pantry Staples for Sushi

Mastering the art of sushi making begins with assembling the essential pantry staples and tools. From perfectly seasoned sushi rice to fresh fish and savory sauces, each ingredient plays a crucial role in crafting authentic and delicious sushi dishes. Whether you're a seasoned sushi chef or a novice enthusiast, having the right ingredients and equipment at your disposal is key to creating sushi rolls that are as impressive as they are flavorful.

Rice Vinegar

Rice vinegar is a fundamental ingredient in sushi rice, imparting its distinct tangy flavor and helping to

achieve the desired texture. It's essential for seasoning the cooked rice to ensure it has the perfect balance of acidity and sweetness.

Adds tanginess to sushi rice.

Balances flavors in the rice.

Gives sushi rice its signature taste.

Essential for achieving the right texture.

Helps in preserving sushi rice for longer periods.

Nori Sheets

Nori sheets are thin, dried seaweed sheets used to wrap sushi rolls. They provide structural integrity to the roll and contribute a subtle oceanic flavor to the overall taste of the sushi.

Wraps the sushi ingredients tightly.

Adds a hint of sea flavor to the sushi.

Provides a crispy texture when toasted.

Essential for making sushi rolls.

Available in different grades for various sushi styles.

Sushi Rice

Sushi rice, also known as shari or sumeshi, is the foundation of sushi. It's a short-grain rice variety seasoned with rice vinegar, sugar, and salt. The sticky texture of sushi rice helps hold the ingredients together in rolls and nigiri.

Sticky texture binds sushi ingredients.

Seasoned with rice vinegar, sugar, and salt.

Forms the base of sushi rolls and nigiri.

Requires precise cooking for optimal results.

Key component for authentic sushi flavor

Soy Sauce

Soy sauce, or shoyu, is a staple condiment in sushi cuisine. It's used both as a dipping sauce for sushi rolls and as a seasoning in various sushi recipes. Soy sauce adds a savory umami flavor that complements the delicate taste of sushi.

Enhances the umami flavor of sushi.

Used as a dipping sauce for sushi rolls.

Adds depth to sushi marinades and sauces.
Available in different varieties like light, dark, and low-sodium.
Essential for enjoying sushi with authentic flavor.

Wasabi

Wasabi, a pungent green paste made from the root of the Wasabia japonica plant, is a traditional accompaniment to sushi. It provides a spicy kick that cuts through the richness of fish and adds complexity to the overall flavor profile of sushi.
Adds a spicy kick to sushi.
Complements the flavor of raw fish.
Enhances the dining experience with its unique heat.
Traditionally served as a condiment with sushi.
Can be mixed into soy sauce for dipping or spread directly on sushi.

Fresh Fish

Fresh fish, such as tuna, salmon, yellowtail, and mackerel, is a crucial ingredient in sushi. It's typically served raw as sashimi or as a topping for nigiri sushi. High-quality, sushi-grade fish should be fresh, flavorful, and free of any off-putting odors.
Served raw as sashimi or nigiri topping.
Requires sushi-grade quality for safety.
Provides essential protein in sushi dishes.
Varied fish types offer diverse flavor profiles.
Freshness is paramount for a superior sushi experience.

Pickled Ginger (Gari)

Pickled ginger, known as gari in Japanese, is thinly sliced ginger pickled in sweet vinegar. It serves as a palate cleanser between different types of sushi, refreshing the taste buds and aiding digestion. Gari also adds a touch of sweetness to balance the savory flavors of sushi.
Cleanses the palate between sushi bites.
Refreshes the taste buds with its tangy flavor.
Aids in digestion after consuming rich fish.
Adds a subtle sweetness to sushi consumption.
Typically served alongside sushi rolls and nigiri.

Sesame Seeds

Sesame seeds are commonly used to garnish sushi rolls, adding a nutty flavor and textural contrast to the dish. They can be toasted to enhance their aroma and flavor before sprinkling them over the sushi rice or rolling them onto the outside of sushi rolls.

Adds nutty flavor and crunch to sushi

Enhances visual appeal as a garnish

Can be toasted for added depth of flavor

Provides textural contrast to soft sushi ingredients

Versatile ingredient for both traditional and creative sushi recipes

Avocado

Avocado has become a popular ingredient in sushi rolls, adding a creamy texture and mild flavor that complements the other components. It's often used in vegetarian sushi rolls or alongside seafood to create balance and richness.

Adds creaminess to sushi rolls.

Provides a mild, buttery flavor.

Popular ingredient in vegetarian sushi.

Complements seafood in sushi rolls.

Rich in healthy fats and nutrients.

Japanese Cucumber

Japanese cucumber, or kyuri, is a staple ingredient in sushi rolls, providing a crisp and refreshing contrast to the other components. It's typically thinly sliced and used as a filling or garnish in sushi rolls to add texture and crunch.

Adds crunch and freshness to sushi.

Provides a refreshing contrast to other ingredients.

Thinly sliced for easy rolling in sushi rolls.

Enhances the visual appeal of sushi dishes.

Offers a light and healthy component to sushi rolls.

Japanese Mayonnaise

Japanese mayonnaise, often referred to as Kewpie mayo, has a distinct flavor and creaminess that complements sushi rolls. It's commonly used as a condiment or mixed into sushi fillings to add richness and depth of flavor.

Adds creaminess and tanginess to sushi.

Distinct flavor compared to traditional mayonnaise.

Common condiment for sushi rolls.

Enhances the richness of sushi fillings.

Available in squeezable bottles for easy application.

Following these essential tips will help you create delicious and authentic sushi right in your own kitchen, mastering the art of this beloved Japanese cuisine.

Choosing the Right Rice

Selecting the right type of rice is vital for making sushi. Opt for short-grain Japanese rice, commonly labeled as sushi rice. Rinse the rice thoroughly until the water runs clear to remove excess starch, which helps in achieving the perfect texture. After cooking, season the rice with a mixture of rice vinegar, sugar, and salt while it's still warm. This step is essential for enhancing the flavor and giving the rice its characteristic sushi taste.

Mastering Rice Preparation

Cook the rice according to the package instructions or using a rice cooker for consistent results. It's essential to maintain the ideal rice-to-water ratio to prevent the rice from being too mushy or too firm. Once cooked, spread the rice evenly on a flat surface, like a wooden sushi rice tub or a shallow tray, to allow excess moisture to evaporate. Gently fan the rice while mixing in the seasoned vinegar to ensure each grain is coated evenly without crushing them.

Slicing Fish and Seafood

When slicing fish for sushi, use a sharp knife with a single, fluid motion to achieve clean cuts. The slices should be uniform in thickness to ensure consistent flavor and texture in every bite. For raw fish, it's essential to use high-quality, sushi-grade fish to minimize the risk of foodborne illness. Additionally, freezing the fish beforehand can help kill any potential parasites.

Perfecting Rolling Techniques

Whether making traditional maki rolls or more intricate sushi creations like nigiri or temaki, mastering the rolling technique is key. Start with a sheet of nori (seaweed) on a bamboo sushi rolling mat, shiny side down. Spread a thin layer of rice evenly over the nori, leaving about a half-inch border at the top edge. Add your desired fillings, such as fish, vegetables, or avocado, then roll tightly using the bamboo mat, applying gentle pressure to shape the sushi.

Presentation and Garnishing

The presentation of sushi is as important as its taste. Use a sharp knife to cut the rolls into uniform pieces, wiping the blade clean between cuts to ensure neat edges. Arrange the sushi pieces on a plate or serving platter, garnishing with pickled ginger, wasabi, and soy sauce for dipping. Add a touch of elegance by incorporating decorative elements like thinly sliced cucumber or sesame seeds for visual appeal.

Chapter 1 Sushi Rice Recipes

Sweet White Sushi Rice

Preparation Time: 10 minutes | Cooking Time: 20 minutes | Servings: 10

Ingredients:

3 cups water
2¼ cups sushi white rice, rinsed
¼ cup rice vinegar

¼ cup white sugar
1¼ teaspoons salt

Preparation:

1. In a medium-sized saucepan, add the water and rice over medium-high heat and bring to a boil. 2. Now adjust the heat to the low and cook, covered for around 15-20 minutes. 3. Meanwhile, in a small-sized saucepan, add oil, vinegar, sugar and salt over medium heat and cook for around 2-3 minutes, stirring continuously. 4. Remove the pan of vinegar mixture from heat and set aside to cool. 5. Remove the pan of rice from heat and set aside, covered for around 10 minutes. 6. In a large-sized glass bowl, add rice and vinegar mixture and gently stir to combine. 7. Set aside. Let cool to room temperature before serving.

Per Serving: Calories 185; Fat: 0g; Sodium 309mg; Total Carbs 42.9g; Fiber 1.6g; Sugars 6.8g; Protein 3.6g

Kombu White Sushi Rice

Preparation Time: 15 minutes | Cooking Time: 10 minutes | Servings: 6

Ingredients:

1¼ cups water
1 cup white sushi rice, rinsed
1 (2-inch) piece kombu
3 tablespoons Japanese rice wine

1 tablespoon mirin
¾ tablespoon white sugar
½ teaspoon sea salt

Preparation:

1. In the pot of Instant Pot, place the water, rice and kombu piece. 2. Close the lid and adjust the vent in seal position. Select "Manual" and cook with "High Pressure" for 2 minutes. 3. Meanwhile, in a small-sized saucepan, add vinegar, oil, sugar and salt over medium heat and cook for around 2-3 minutes, stirring continuously. 4. Remove the pan of vinegar mixture from heat and set aside to cool. 5. After cooking time is completed, press "Cancel" and do a "Natural" release for 8 minutes. Then do a "Quick" release. 6. Carefully open the lid and stir the mixture. 7. In a large-sized glass bowl, add rice and vinegar mixture and gently stir to combine. 7. Set aside to cool to room temperature before serving.

Per Serving: Calories 149; Total fat 0g; Sodium 206mg; Total Carbs 31.9g; Fiber 1.2g; Sugars 3.6g; Protein 2.9g

Steamed White Sushi Rice

Preparation Time: 10 minutes | Cooking Time: 30 minutes | Servings: 4

Ingredients:

2 cups short-grain white rice, rinsed
¼ cup white sugar
½ cup rice wine vinegar

2 tablespoons mirin
1 teaspoon salt

Preparation:

1. In a large-sized bowl of water, place the rice. 2. Cover the bowl and set it aside to soak for 2-8 hours. 3. Then drain the rice thoroughly. 4. Line the bottom basket of a bamboo steamer with a clean damp kitchen cloth. 5. Carefully place the rice over the cloth. 6. Now, place another damp kitchen cloth on top of the rice. 7. Carefully fold the corners of cloth towards the center. 8. Cover the basket with its lid. 9. Fill a large-sized wok with water about halfway and bring to a boil. 10. Place the steamer into the wok. 11. Steam the rice for around 30 minutes. (Make sure that water has not evaporated during the cooking process). 12. Meanwhile, in a small-sized saucepan, add vinegar, oil, sugar and salt over medium heat and cook for around 2-3 minutes, stirring continuously. 13. Remove the pan of vinegar mixture from heat and set aside to cool. 14. In a large-sized glass bowl, add rice and vinegar mixture and gently stir to combine. 15. Set aside to cool to room temperature before serving.

Per Serving: Calories 284; Total fat 0.5g; Sodium 972mg; Total Carbs 66.6g; Fiber 0.6g; Sugars 18g; Protein 3.6g

Homemade Sushi Brown Rice

Preparation Time: 10 minutes | Cooking Time: 40 minutes | Servings: 4

Ingredients:

3 cups water
2 cups short-grain brown rice, rinsed
2 teaspoons salt

3½ ounce rice vinegar
3 teaspoons white sugar

Preparation:

1. In a large-sized bowl of water, soak the rice for around 2 hours. 2. Then drain the rice thoroughly. 3. In a large-sized saucepan, add the water and rice over high heat and bring to a boil. 4. Now adjust to low heat and cook, covered for around 35 minutes. 5. Remove the pan of rice from heat and set aside, covered for around 15 minutes. 6. Meanwhile, in a small-sized microwave-safe bowl, add vinegar, sugar and salt and microwave on high for around 30-45 seconds. 7. In a large-sized glass bowl, add rice and vinegar mixture and gently stir to combine. 8. Set aside to cool to room temperature before serving.

Per Serving: Calories 155; Total fat 0.9g; Sodium 916mg; Total Carbs 33.9g; Fiber 2.6g; Sugars 5.3.6g; Protein 3.3g

Basic White Sushi Rice

Preparation Time: 10 minutes | Cooking Time: 30 minutes | Servings: 12

Ingredients:

3 cups medium grain white rice
3¼ cups water

⅓ cup seasoned rice vinegar

Preparation:

1. Place the rice in the pot of rice cooker and top with water. 2. Cover the pot with lid and cook according to manufacturer's instructions. 3. After cooking time is finished, switch off the cooker and let it steam for around 15 minutes before opening the lid. 4. Open the lid and with a fork, fluff the rice. 5. In a large-sized glass bowl, add rice and vinegar and gently stir to combine. 6. Set aside to cool to room temperature before serving.

Per Serving: Calories 177; Total fat 0.4g; Sodium 186mg; Total Carbs 39.2g; Fiber 1.3g; Sugars 1.6g; Protein 3.5g

Chapter 2 Sushi Rice Roll Recipes

Avocado Sushi Rolls

Preparation Time: 15 minutes | Servings: 4

Ingredients:

4 nori sheets
4 cups cooked and seasoned sushi rice cooled

2 ripe avocados, peeled, pitted and sliced

Preparation:

1. Place 1 large-sized piece of plastic wrap onto a smooth surface. 2. Arrange 1 bamboo sushi mat over the plastic wrap. 3. Place 1 nori sheet on mat, shining-side-down, with the longer side of the nori facing you. 4. Place about 1 cup of rice over the nori, leaving a 1-inch border. 5. With your wet fingers, gently press the rice onto the nori in an even layer. 6. Arrange the slices of avocado across the center of the rice. 7. Carefully lift up the bottom edge of the sushi mat and then fold it over the filling into a roll. 8. With the sushi mat, squeeze the roll tightly. 9. Carefully remove the mat and plastic wrap. 10. Repeat with remaining nori sheet and filling. 11. With a wet knife, cut each roll into bite-sized pieces. Serve with your favorite dipping sauce.

Per Serving: Calories 343; Total fat 8.4g; Sodium 125mg; Total Carbs 62.9g; Fiber 6.1g; Sugars 0.6g; Protein 6.1g

Mango, Avocado & Greens Sushi Rolls

Preparation Time: 15 minutes | Servings: 4

Ingredients:

1 ripe mango, peeled, pitted and cut into vertical strips
1 avocado, peeled, pitted and sliced
1 cucumber, cut into long strips
½ cup micro greens

2 tablespoons sesame seeds
4 nori sheets
4 cups cooked and seasoned sushi rice (cooled)

Preparation:

1. In a bowl, add the mango, avocado, cucumber, greens and sesame seeds and blend to incorporate thoroughly. 2. Place 1 large-sized piece of plastic wrap onto a smooth surface. 3. Arrange 1 bamboo sushi mat over the plastic wrap. 4. Place 1 nori sheet on mat, shining-side-down, with the longer side of the nori facing you. 5. Place about 1 cup of rice over the nori, leaving a 1-inch border. 6. With your wet fingers, gently press the rice onto the nori in an even layer. 7. Sprinkle the rice with sesame seeds. 8. Arrange the mango mixture across the center of the rice. 9. Carefully lift up the bottom edge of the sushi mat and then fold it over the filling into a roll. 10. With the sushi mat, squeeze the roll tightly. 11. Carefully remove the mat and plastic wrap. 12. Repeat with remaining nori sheet and filling. 13. With a wet knife, cut each roll into bite-sized pieces. Serve with your favorite dipping sauce.

Per Serving: Calories 178; Total fat 12.8g; Sodium 6mg; Total Carbs 61.2g; Fiber 6g; Sugars 8.6g; Protein 7.4g

Avocado & Cucumber Sushi Rolls

Preparation Time: 15 minutes | Servings: 4

Ingredients:

4 nori sheets
4 cups cooked and seasoned sushi rice (cooled)

½ of medium cucumber, cut into thin strips
1 medium avocado, peeled, pitted and sliced

Preparation:

1. Place 1 large-sized piece of plastic wrap onto a smooth surface. 2. Arrange 1 bamboo sushi mat over the plastic wrap. 3. Place 1 nori sheet on mat, shining-side-down, with the longer side of the nori facing you. 4. Place about 1 cup of rice over the nori, leaving a 1-inch border. 5. With your wet fingers, gently press the rice onto the nori in an even layer. 6. Arrange the slices of cucumber and avocado across the center of the rice. 7. Carefully lift up the bottom edge of the sushi mat and then fold it over the filling into a roll. 8. With the sushi mat, squeeze the roll tightly. 9. Carefully remove the mat and plastic wrap. 10. Repeat with remaining nori sheets and filling. 11. With a wet knife, cut each roll into bite-sized pieces. Serve with your favorite dipping sauce.

Per Serving: Calories 227; Total fat 10g; Sodium 6mg; Total Carbs 31.8g; Fiber 3.8g; Sugars 0.6g; Protein 3.5g

Asparagus & Prosciutto Sushi Rolls

Preparation Time: 15 minutes | Cooking Time: 4 minutes | Servings: 2

Ingredients:

2 asparagus spears
2 cups cooked and seasoned sushi rice (cooled)
2 nori sheets

2 ounces goat cheese, crumbled
4 prosciutto slices, thinly sliced

Preparation:

1. In a small-sized saucepan of boiling water, add the asparagus spears and cook for around 3-4 minutes. 2. Drain the water and immediately plunge the asparagus spears into a bowl of ice water. 3. After cooling, drain the asparagus spears and with paper towels pat dry them. 4. Place 1 large-sized piece of plastic wrap onto a smooth surface. 5. Arrange 1 bamboo sushi mat over the plastic wrap. 6. Place 1 nori sheet on mat, shining-side-down, with the longer side of the nori facing you. 7. Place about 1 cup of rice over the nori, leaving a 1-inch border. 8. With your wet fingers, gently press the rice onto the nori in an even layer. 9. Arrange the asparagus, cheese pieces and prosciutto slices across the center of the rice. 10. Carefully lift up the bottom edge of the sushi mat and then fold it over the filling into a roll. 11. With the sushi mat, squeeze the roll tightly. 12. Carefully remove the mat and plastic wrap. 13. Repeat with remaining nori sheet and filling. 14. With a wet knife, cut each roll into bite-sized pieces. Serve with your favorite dipping sauce.

Per Serving: Calories 392; Total fat 8.6g; Sodium 986mg; Total Carbs 55.2g; Fiber 1.6g; Sugars 13.6g; Protein 21.2g

Alfalfa Sprout & Red Pepper Sushi Rolls

Preparation Time: 15 minutes | Servings: 4

Ingredients:

4 nori sheets
4 cups cooked and seasoned sushi brown rice (cooled)
1 cup Alfalfa sprouts

1 roasted red pepper, sliced
1 cup carrots, peeled and thinly sliced
1 cup cucumber, thinly sliced

Preparation:

1. Place 1 large-sized piece of plastic wrap onto a smooth surface. 2. Arrange 1 bamboo sushi mat over the plastic wrap. 3. Place 1 nori sheet on mat, shining-side-down, with the longer side of the nori facing you. 4. Place about 1 cup of rice over the nori, leaving a 1-inch border. 5. With your wet fingers, gently press the rice onto the nori in an even layer. 6. Arrange the sprouts, red pepper, carrot and cucumber across the center of the rice. 7. Carefully lift up the bottom edge of the sushi mat and then fold it over the filling into a roll. 8. With the sushi mat, squeeze the roll tightly. 9. Carefully remove the mat and plastic wrap. 10. Repeat with remaining nori sheets and filling. 11. With a wet knife, cut each roll into bite-sized pieces. Serve with your favorite dipping sauce.

Per Serving: Calories 275; Total fat 3.4g; Sodium 456mg; Total Carbs 56.9g; Fiber 2.6g; Sugars 10.6g; Protein 9.2g

Spam Sushi Rolls

Preparation Time: 15 minutes | Servings: 5

Ingredients:

5 nori sheets
5 cups cooked white rice
1 (12-ounce) can spam, cut into ½-inch strips and fried

5 tablespoons mayonnaise
1 cucumbers, cut into strips

Preparation:

1. Place 1 large-sized piece of plastic wrap onto a smooth surface. 2. Arrange 1 bamboo sushi mat over the plastic wrap. 3. Place 1 nori sheet on mat, shining-side-down, with the longer side of the nori facing you. 4. Place about 1 cup of rice over the nori, leaving a 1-inch border. 5. With your wet fingers, gently press the rice onto the nori in an even layer. 6. Spread the mayonnaise over the rice. 7. Arrange the spam and cucumber across the center of the rice. 8. Carefully lift up the bottom edge of the sushi mat and then fold it over the filling into a roll. 9. With the sushi mat, squeeze the roll tightly. 10. Carefully remove the mat and plastic wrap. 11. Repeat with remaining nori sheets and filling. 12. With a wet knife, cut each roll into bite-sized pieces. Serve with your favorite dipping sauce.

Per Serving: Calories 375; Total fat 22.4g; Sodium 786mg; Total Carbs 46.9g; Fiber 0.6g; Sugars 3.6g; Protein 12.4g

Salmon & Cashew Sushi Rolls

Preparation Time: 15 minutes | Servings: 2

Ingredients:

2 nori sheets
2 cups hot cooked white rice
1 tablespoons rice vinegar
1 tablespoon white sugar
Pinch of salt

2 teaspoons garlic, crushed
½ cup cashews, crushed
2 scallions, finely cut up
3 ounces cold cream cheese, cut into thin strips
2 ounces smoked salmon, cut into strips

Preparation:

1. In a large-sized bowl, add the cooked rice, vinegar, sugar and salt and blend to incorporate thoroughly. 2. Set aside to cool thoroughly. 3. Place 1 large-sized piece of plastic wrap onto a smooth surface. 4. Arrange 1 bamboo sushi mat over the plastic wrap. 5. Place 1 nori sheet on mat, shining -side-down, with the longer side of the nori facing you. 6. Place about 1 cup of rice over the nori, leaving a 1-inch border. 7. With your wet fingers, gently press the rice onto the nori in an even layer. 8. Sprinkle the rice with garlic, cashews and scallions. 9. Arrange the slices of cream cheese and salmon across the center of the rice. 10. Carefully lift up the bottom edge of the sushi mat and then fold it over the filling into a roll. 11. With the sushi mat, squeeze the roll tightly. 12. Carefully remove the mat and plastic wrap. 13. Repeat with remaining nori sheet and filling. 14. With a wet knife, cut each roll into bite-size pieces and serve with your favorite dipping sauce.

Per Serving: Calories 590; Total fat 32.4g; Sodium 791mg; Total Carbs 60.2g; Fiber 2.1g; Sugars 8.4g; Protein 17.5g

Flounder Sushi Rolls

Preparation Time: 15 minutes | Servings: 4

Ingredients:

4 nori sheets
4 ounces yellowtail flounder, cut into ¼-inch cubes
¼ cup mayonnaise

1 tablespoon Sriracha
4 cups cooked and seasoned sushi rice (cooled)
¼ medium cucumber, peeled and julienned

Preparation:

1. In a medium-sized bowl, add flounder cubes, mayonnaise and Sriracha and blend to incorporate. 2. Place 1 large-sized piece of plastic wrap onto a smooth surface. 3. Arrange 1 bamboo sushi mat over the plastic wrap. 4. Place 1 nori sheet on mat, shining-side-down, with the longer side of the nori facing you. 5. Place about 1 cup of rice over the nori, leaving a 1-inch border. 6. With your wet fingers, gently press the rice onto the nori in an even layer. 7. Arrange the flounder cubes and slices of cucumber across the center of the rice. 8. Carefully lift up the bottom edge of the sushi mat and then fold it over the filling into a roll. 9. With the sushi mat, squeeze the roll tightly. 10. Carefully remove the mat and plastic wrap. 11. Repeat with remaining nori sheet and filling. 12. With a wet knife, cut each roll into bite-sized pieces. Serve with your favorite dipping sauce.

Per Serving: Calories 342; Total fat 22.4g; Sodium 196mg; Total Carbs 58.9g; Fiber 0.8g; Sugars 1.1g; Protein 12g

Cucumber Sushi Rolls

Preparation Time: 15 minutes | Servings: 4

Ingredients:

4 nori sheets
4 cups cooked and seasoned sushi rice (cooled)

1 cucumber, cut into strips
3-4 teaspoons sesame seeds, toasted

Preparation:

1. Place 1 large-sized piece of plastic wrap onto a smooth surface. 2. Arrange 1 bamboo sushi mat over the plastic wrap. 3. Place 1 nori sheet on mat, shining-side-down, with the longer side of the nori facing you. 4. Place about 1 cup of rice over the nori, leaving a 1-inch border. 5. With your wet fingers, gently press the rice onto the nori in an even layer. 6. Sprinkle the rice with sesame seeds. 7. Arrange the slices of cucumber across the center of the rice. 8. Carefully lift up the bottom edge of the sushi mat and then fold it over the filling into a roll. 9. With the sushi mat, squeeze the roll tightly. 10. Carefully remove the mat and plastic wrap. 11. Repeat with remaining nori sheets and filling. 12. With a wet knife, cut each roll into bite-sized pieces. Serve with your favorite dipping sauce.

Per Serving: Calories 233; Total Fat 1.2g; Sodium 425mg; Total Carbs 63.9g; Fiber 2.1g; Sugars 3.6g; Protein 5.9g

Veggie & Kimchi Sushi Rolls

Preparation Time: 15 minutes | Servings: 3

Ingredients:

3 cups hot cooked sushi rice
1 tablespoon seasoned rice vinegar
1 tablespoon agave nectar
3 nori sheets

½ cup kimchi
¼ cup carrots, peeled and shredded
½ of cucumber peeled, seeded and cut into strips
½ of avocado, peeled, pitted and cut into strips

Preparation:

1. In a bowl, add the rice, agave nectar and vinegar and toss to incorporate. 2. Set aside to cool thoroughly. 3. Place 1 large-sized piece of plastic wrap onto a smooth surface. 4. Arrange 1 bamboo sushi mat over the plastic wrap. 5. Place 1 nori sheet on mat, shining-side-down, with the longer side of the nori facing you. 6. Place 1 cup of rice over the nori, leaving a 1-inch border. 7. With your wet fingers, gently press the rice onto the nori in an even layer. 8. Arrange the kimchi, carrots, cucumber and avocado across the center of the rice. 9. Carefully lift up the bottom edge of the sushi mat and then fold it over the filling into a roll. 10. With the sushi mat, squeeze the roll tightly. 11. Carefully remove the mat and plastic wrap. 12. Repeat with remaining nori sheet and filling. 13. With a wet knife, cut each roll into bite-sized pieces. Serve with your favorite dipping sauce.

Per Serving: Calories 324; Total fat 6.4g; Sodium 126mg; Total Carbs 62.9g; Fiber 5.9g; Sugars 7.6g; Protein 7.2g

Ground Beef & Veggie Sushi Rolls

Preparation Time: 15 minutes | Cooking Time: 20 minutes | Servings: 8

Ingredients:

For the Beef:
1-pound ground beef
1 scallion, sliced
2 cloves garlic, finely cut up
For the Veggies & Eggs:
½ large cucumber peeled and cut into long, thin strips
3 large eggs
Salt, as desired
For the Rice:
8 cups hot cooked sushi rice
2 teaspoons toasted sesame oil
For the Rolls:
8 nori sheets

2 tablespoons mirin
2 tablespoon soy sauce
1 teaspoon sesame oil

2 tablespoons vegetable oil
2-3 carrots, peeled and cut into long, thin strips
3 cups baby spinach

¾ teaspoon unrefined salt

Preparation:

1. For the beef: in a bowl, add all ingredients and blend to incorporate thoroughly. Set aside for around10-15 minutes. 2. For the veggies: Heat a medium-sized pot of water until it boils. Put the spinach in and let it cook for one minute. Then, drain it using a fine-mesh strainer and cool it under cold running water. Press out as much water as possible. Season with salt to your liking and set it aside. 3. Arrange the cucumber slices on a large-sized plate and sprinkle with salt. Set aside for around 10 minutes. 4. With your hands, squeeze the cucumber to release the liquid. Set aside. 5. In a small-sized bowl, whisk together the eggs and salt. 6. In a 10-inch cast-iron wok, heat oil over high heat. 7. Add the eggs and immediately turn down the heat to low. 8. Cook for around 3-4 minutes, flipping once. 9. Remove the cooked eggs from heat and place onto a cutting board. 10. Cut the cooked egg into strips and set aside. 11. In the same wok, hear remaining oil and cook the carrots with a little salt for around 3-5 minutes. 12. Transfer the carrot onto a plate. 13. In the same wok, add the beef and cook for around 8-10 minutes. 14. Transfer the beef onto a plate and set aside to cool. 15. In a large bowl, add hot rice, sesame oil and salt and blend to incorporate. Set aside to cool. 16. Place 1 large-sized piece of plastic wrap onto a smooth surface. 17. Arrange 1 bamboo sushi mat over the plastic wrap. 18. Place 1 nori sheet on mat, shining-side-down, with the longer side of the nori facing you. 19. Place about 1 cup of rice over the nori, leaving a 1-inch border. 20. With your wet fingers, gently press the rice onto the nori in an even layer. 21. Arrange the cooked beef, egg strips, cucumber, carrot and spinach across the center of the rice. 22. Carefully lift up the bottom edge of the sushi mat and then fold it over the filling into a roll. 23. With the sushi mat, squeeze the roll tightly. 24. Carefully remove the mat and plastic wrap. 25. Repeat with remaining nori sheet and filling. 26. With a wet knife, cut each roll into bite-sized pieces. Serve with your favorite dipping sauce.

Per Serving: Calories 392; Total fat 9.4g; Sodium 396mg; Total Carbs 45.7g; Fiber 1.8g; Sugars 4.6g; Protein 30.4g

Beef Steak Sushi Rolls

Preparation Time: 15 minutes | Cooking Time: 5 minutes | Servings: 6

Ingredients:

½ pound beef steak, thinly sliced
6 cups cooked and seasoned sushi rice
6 nori sheets

1 carrot, peeled and julienned
1 cucumber, julienned
1 avocado, peeled, pitted and sliced

Preparation:

1. Heat a greased wok over medium heat and cook the steak strips for around 4-5 minutes. 2. Remove from heat and set aside to cool. 3. Place 1 large-sized piece of plastic wrap onto a smooth surface. 4. Arrange 1 bamboo sushi mat over the plastic wrap. 5. Place 1 nori sheet on mat, shining-side-down, with the longer side of the nori facing you. 6. Place about 1 cup of rice over the nori, leaving a 1-inch border. 7. With your wet fingers, gently press the rice onto the nori in an even layer. 8. Arrange the cooked steak strips, carrot, cucumber and avocado across the center of the rice. 9. Carefully lift up the bottom edge of the sushi mat and then fold it over the filling into a roll. 10. With the sushi mat, squeeze the roll tightly. 11. Carefully remove the mat and plastic wrap. 12. Repeat with remaining nori sheet and filling. 13. With a wet knife, cut each roll into bite-sized pieces. Serve with your favorite dipping sauce.

Per Serving: Calories 484; Total fat 16.4g; Sodium 689mg; Total Carbs 78.9g; Fiber 5.6g; Sugars 9.6g; Protein 20.2g

Chicken & Celery Sushi Rolls

Preparation Time: 15 minutes | Servings: 4

Ingredients:

½ pound cooked chicken breast tenderloins
¼ cup hot pepper sauce
4 nori sheets

4 cups cooked and seasoned sushi rice (cooled)
1 carrot, peeled and cut into matchsticks
1 celery stalk, cut into matchsticks

Preparation:

1. In a bowl, add chicken strips and hot sauce and toss to incorporate. 2. Place 1 large-sized piece of plastic wrap onto a smooth surface. 3. Arrange 1 bamboo sushi mat over the plastic wrap. 4. Place 1 nori sheet on mat, shining-side-down, with the longer side of the nori facing you. 5. Place about 1 cup of rice over the nori, leaving a 1-inch border. 6. With your wet fingers, gently press the rice onto the nori in an even layer. 7. Arrange the slices of chicken, carrot and celery across the center of the rice. 8. Carefully lift up the bottom edge of the sushi mat and then fold it over the filling into a roll. 9. With the sushi mat, squeeze the roll tightly. 10. Carefully remove the mat and plastic wrap. 11. Repeat with remaining nori sheets and filling. 12. With a wet knife, cut each roll into bite-sized pieces. Serve with your favorite dipping sauce.

Per Serving: Calories 338; Total fat 2.2g; Sodium 456mg; Total Carbs 55.4g; Fiber 1g; Sugars 1.3; Protein 21.6g

Delicious Beef & Bell Pepper Sushi Rolls

Preparation Time: 15 minutes | Servings: 4

Ingredients:

4 nori sheets
4 cups cooked and seasoned sushi rice (cooled)
10 ounces cooked beef, cut into long thin strips

1 cup bell pepper, seeded and cut into thin strips
¼ cup Asian dressing

Preparation:

1. Place 1 large-sized piece of plastic wrap onto a smooth surface. 2. Arrange 1 bamboo sushi mat over the plastic wrap. 3. Place 1 nori sheet on mat, shining-side-down, with the longer side of the nori facing you. 4. Place about 1 cup of rice over the nori, leaving a 1-inch border. 5. With your wet fingers, gently press the rice onto the nori in an even layer. 6. Arrange the slices of beef and bell pepper across the center of the rice. 7. Drizzle each with 1 tablespoon dressing8. Carefully lift up the bottom edge of the sushi mat and then fold it over the filling into a roll. 9. With the sushi mat, squeeze the roll tightly. 10. Carefully remove the mat and plastic wrap. 11. Repeat with remaining nori sheets and filling. 12. With a wet knife, cut each roll into bite-sized pieces. Serve with your favorite dipping sauce.

Per Serving: Calories 248; Total fat 5.8g; Sodium 125mg; Total Carbs 45.6g; Fiber 1.9g; Sugars 1.9g; Protein 26.8g

Salmon & Cream Cheese Sushi Rolls

Preparation Time: 15 minutes | Servings: 2

Ingredients:

⅓ cup cream cheese, softened
1 tablespoon red onion, finely cut up
2 nori sheets

2 cups cooked and seasoned sushi rice (cooled)
2 tablespoons sesame seeds, toasted
⅓ cup smoked salmon

Preparation:

1. In a bowl, mix together the cream cheese and onion. 2. Arrange 1 bamboo sushi mat over the plastic wrap. 3. Place 1 nori sheet on mat, shining-side-down, with the longer side of the nori facing you. 4. Place about 1 cup of rice over the nori, leaving a 1-inch border. 5. With your wet fingers, gently press the rice onto the nori in an even layer. 6. Sprinkle the rice with sesame seeds. 7. Place the salmon over the rice across the center of the rice. 8. Place the cream cheese mixture along the edge of salmon slices9. Carefully lift up the bottom edge of the sushi mat and then fold it over the filling into a roll. 10. With the sushi mat, squeeze the roll tightly. 11. Carefully remove the mat and plastic wrap. 12. Repeat with remaining nori sheet and filling. 13. With a wet knife, cut each roll into bite-sized pieces and top with remaining BBQ sauce and cheese. 14. Serve with your favorite dipping sauce.

Per Serving: Calories 334; Total fat 15.4g; Sodium 329mg; Total Carbs 38.9g; Fiber 2.1g; Sugars 1.9g; Protein 10.9g

Salmon, Daikon Sprouts & Jicama Sushi Rolls

Preparation Time: 15 minutes | Cooking Time: 5 minutes | Servings: 8

Ingredients:

1 cup rice wine vinegar
¼ cup mirin
½ cup sugar
8 cups hot cooked sushi rice
8 nori sheets

1 cup smoked salmon, cut into strips
1 cup jicama, cut into strips
1 cup daikon sprouts
¼ cup pickled ginger, julienned
2-3 teaspoons wasabi oil

Preparation:

1. For the rice: in a small-sized saucepan, add vinegar, sugar and salt over low heat and cook for around 3-5 minutes, stirring frequently. In a large-sized bowl, add the cooked rice and vinegar mixture and toss to incorporate. Set aside to cool thoroughly. 2. Place 1 large-sized piece of plastic wrap onto a smooth surface. 3. Arrange 1 bamboo sushi mat over the plastic wrap. 4. Place 1 nori sheet on mat, shining-side-down, with the longer side of the nori facing you. 5. Place about 1 cup of rice over the nori, leaving a 1-inch border. 6. With your wet fingers, gently press the rice onto the nori in an even layer. 7. Arrange the salmon, jicama, sprouts and ginger, julienned across the center of the rice. Drizzle the top with wasabi oil. 8. Carefully lift up the bottom edge of the sushi mat and then fold it over the filling into a roll. 9. With the sushi mat, squeeze the roll tightly. 10. Carefully remove the mat and plastic wrap. 11. Repeat with remaining nori sheets and filling. 12. With a wet knife, cut each roll into bite-sized pieces. Serve with your favorite dipping sauce.

Per Serving: Calories 430; Total Fat 2.1g; Sodium 513mg; Total Carbs 87.6g; Fiber 3.8g; Sugars 2.6g; Protein 13g

Salmon, Cucumber & Carrot Sushi Rolls

Preparation Time: 15 minutes | Servings: 2

Ingredients:

2 nori sheets
1 cup cooked and seasoned sushi rice (cooled)
½ cup smoked salmon, thinly sliced

½ of small carrot, peeled and cut into thin strips
1 small cucumber, cut into thin strips

Preparation:

1. Place 1 large-sized piece of plastic wrap onto a smooth surface. 2. Arrange 1 bamboo sushi mat over the plastic wrap. 3. Place 1 nori sheet on mat, shining-side-down, with the longer side of the nori facing you. 4. Place about 1 cup of rice over the nori, leaving a 1-inch border. 5. With your wet fingers, gently press the rice onto the nori in an even layer. 6. Arrange the slices of salmon, carrot and cucumber across the center of the rice. 7. Carefully lift up the bottom edge of the sushi mat and then fold it over the filling into a roll. 8. With the sushi mat, squeeze the roll tightly. 9. Carefully remove the mat and plastic wrap. 10. Repeat with remaining nori sheets and filling. 11. With a wet knife, cut each roll into bite-sized pieces. Serve with your favorite dipping sauce.

Per Serving: Calories 191; Total fat 17.4g; Sodium 286mg; Total Carbs 34.9g; Fiber 1.6g; Sugars 3.6g; Protein 10.2g

Cheese Ham Sushi Rolls

Preparation Time: 15 minutes | Cooking Time: 4 minutes | Servings: 4

Ingredients:

4 cups cooked sushi rice (cooled)
1 teaspoon olive oil
4 nori sheets
1 carrot, peeled and cut into thin strips
4 American cheese slices, cut into thin strips

1 tablespoon sesame oil
Salt, as desired
2 eggs, whisked
4 cooked ham slices, cut into thin strips
1 cucumber, peeled and cut into thin strips

Preparation:

1. In a large-sized bowl, add cooked rice, sesame oil and salt and toss to incorporate thoroughly. Set aside. 2. In a frying pan, heat oil olive oil over medium-high heat. 3. Add eggs and cook for around 3-4 minutes or until set thoroughly, flipping once halfway through. 4. Remove the cooked eggs from the heat place onto a cutting board. 5. Cut the cooked egg into strips and set aside. 6. Place 1 large-sized piece of plastic wrap onto a smooth surface. 7. Arrange 1 bamboo sushi mat over the plastic wrap. 8. Place 1 nori sheet on mat, shining-side-down, with the longer side of the nori facing you. 9. Place about 1 cup of rice over the nori, leaving a 1-inch border. 10. With your wet fingers, gently press the rice onto the nori in an even layer. 11. Arrange the slices of ham, carrot, cucumber, eggs and cheese across the center of the rice. 12. Carefully lift up the bottom edge of the sushi mat and then fold it over the filling into a roll. 13. With the sushi mat, squeeze the roll tightly. 14. Carefully remove the mat and plastic wrap.

Per Serving: Calories 374; Total fat 18.4g; Sodium 617mg; Total Carbs 48.9g; Fiber 1.9g; Sugars 3.1g; Protein 15.2g

Garlic Shrimp & Avocado Sushi Rolls

Preparation Time: 15 minutes | Cooking Time: 5 minutes | Servings: 5

Ingredients:

1 tablespoon butter
1 clove garlic, crushed
8 large shrimp, peeled and deveined
5 nori sheets

5 cups cooked and seasoned sushi rice (cooled)
1 cucumber, cut into thin strips
1 avocado, peeled, pitted sliced thinly

Preparation:

1. In a small-sized wok, melt butter over medium heat and sauté the garlic for around 1 minute. 2. Add the shrimp and cook for around 3-4 minutes. 3. Remove the wok of shrimp from heat and set aside to cool. 4. Then cut the shrimp into small pieces. 5. Place 1 large-sized piece of plastic wrap onto a smooth surface. 6. Arrange 1 bamboo sushi mat over the plastic wrap. 7. Place 1 nori sheet on mat, shining-side-down, with the longer side of the nori facing you. 8. Place about 1 cup of rice over the nori, leaving a 1-inch border. 9. With your wet fingers, gently press the rice onto the nori in an even layer. 10. Arrange the shrimp, slices of cucumber and avocado across the center of the rice. 11. Carefully lift up the bottom edge of the sushi mat and then fold it over the filling into a roll. 12. With the sushi mat, squeeze the roll tightly. 13. Carefully remove the mat and plastic wrap. 14. Repeat with remaining nori sheets and filling. 15. With a wet knife, cut each roll into bite-sized pieces. Serve with your favorite dipping sauce.

Per Serving: Calories 390; Total fat 11.6g; Sodium 124mg; Total Carbs 59.9g; Fiber 3.8g; Sugars 1.2g; Protein 15.1g

Shrimp Tempura Sushi Rolls

Preparation Time: 15 minutes | Servings: 4

Ingredients:

8 cooked shrimp tempura
4 nori sheets
4 cups cooked and seasoned sushi rice (cooled)

8 cucumber strips
3 tablespoons sesame seeds

Preparation:

1. Place 1 large-sized piece of plastic wrap onto a smooth surface. 2. Arrange 1 bamboo sushi mat over the plastic wrap. 3. Place 1 nori sheet on mat, shining-side-down, with the longer side of the nori facing you. 4. Place about 1 cup of rice over the nori, leaving a 1-inch border. 5. With your wet fingers, gently press the rice onto the nori in an even layer. 6. Sprinkle the rice with sesame seeds. 7. Arrange the shrimp tempura and slices of cucumber across the center of the rice. 8. Carefully lift up the bottom edge of the sushi mat and then fold it over the filling into a roll. 9. With the sushi mat, squeeze the roll tightly. 10. Carefully remove the mat and plastic wrap. 11. Repeat with remaining nori sheet and filling. 12. With a wet knife, cut each roll into bite-sized pieces. Serve with your favorite dipping sauce.

Per Serving: Calories 573; Total fat 26.3g; Sodium 1003mg; Total Carbs 53.5g; Fiber 6.7g; Sugars 7.3g; Protein 22.9g

Tuna Sushi Rolls

Preparation Time: 15 minutes | Servings: 4

Ingredients:

8 ounces sashimi-grade tuna, cut into ¼-inch cubes
2 scallions, cut into thin rounds
4 tablespoons mayonnaise
1 tablespoon hot chile sauce

4 nori sheets
4 cups cooked and seasoned sushi rice (cooled)
1 tablespoon sesame seeds, toasted

Preparation:

1. In a medium-sized bowl, add tuna, scallions, mayonnaise and hot sauce and blend to incorporate thoroughly. 2. Place 1 large-sized piece of plastic wrap onto a smooth surface. 3. Arrange 1 bamboo sushi mat over the plastic wrap. 4. Place 1 nori sheet on mat, shining-side-down, with the longer side of the nori facing you. 5. Place about 1 cup of rice over the nori, leaving a 1-inch border. 6. With your wet fingers, gently press the rice onto the nori in an even layer. 7. Sprinkle the rice with sesame seeds. 8. Arrange the tuna pieces across the center of the rice. 9. Carefully lift up the bottom edge of the sushi mat and then fold it over the filling into a roll. 10. With the sushi mat, squeeze the roll tightly. 11. Carefully remove the mat and plastic wrap. 12. Repeat with remaining nori sheet and filling. 13. With a wet knife, cut each roll into bite-sized pieces. Serve with your favorite dipping sauce.

Per Serving: Calories 350; Total fat 14.4g; Sodium 116mg; Total Carbs 40.9g; Fiber 1.6g; Sugars 1g; Protein 18.2g

---

Tuna & Avocado Sushi Rolls

Preparation Time: 15 minutes | Servings: 3

Ingredients:

6 ounces sashimi-grade yellowfin tuna, cut into small chunks
1 scallion, cut up
⅓ cup mayonnaise
3 tablespoons chile oil
1 tablespoon sesame oil

3 nori sheets
3 cups cooked and seasoned sushi rice (cooled)
¼ English cucumber, cut into matchsticks
½ ripe avocado, peeled, pitted and thinly sliced

Preparation:

1. In a medium-sized bowl, add tuna, scallion, mayonnaise, chile oil, sesame oil and Sriracha and with a fork, mix to incorporate thoroughly. 2. Place 1 large-sized piece of plastic wrap onto a smooth surface. 3. Arrange 1 bamboo sushi mat over the plastic wrap. 4. Place 1 nori sheet on mat, shining -side-down, with the longer side of the nori facing you. 5. Place about 1 cup of rice over the nori, leaving a 1-inch border. 6. With your wet fingers, gently press the rice onto the nori in an even layer. 7. Arrange the tuna chunks and slices of cucumber and avocado across the center of the rice. 8. Carefully lift up the bottom edge of the sushi mat and then fold it over the filling into a roll. 9. With the sushi mat, squeeze the roll tightly. 10. Carefully remove the mat and plastic wrap. 11. Repeat with remaining nori sheet and filling. 12. With a wet knife, cut each roll into bite-size pieces and serve with your favorite dipping sauce.

Per Serving: Calories 686; Total fat 38.9g; Sodium 1086mg; Total Carbs 64g; Fiber 3.6g; Sugars 3.6g; Protein 21.3g

---

Crab & Avocado Sushi Rolls

Preparation Time: 15 minutes | Servings: 4

Ingredients:

4 nori sheets
4 cups cooked and seasoned sushi rice (cooled)
3 tablespoons sesame seeds, toasted

1 cucumber, seeded and thinly sliced into long strips
1 small avocado, peeled, pitted and thinly sliced
4 imitation crabmeat sticks, sliced in half lengthwise

Preparation:

1.Place 1 large-sized piece of plastic wrap onto a smooth surface. 2. Arrange 1 bamboo sushi mat over the plastic wrap. 3. Place 1 nori sheet on mat, shining-side-down, with the longer side of the nori facing you. 4. Place about 1 cup of rice over the nori, leaving a 1-inch border. 5. With your wet fingers, gently press the rice onto the nori in an even layer. 6. Sprinkle the rice with sesame seeds. 7. Arrange the cucumber, avocado and crabmeat across the center of the rice. 8. Carefully lift up the bottom edge of the sushi mat and then fold it over the filling into a roll. 9. With the sushi mat, squeeze the roll tightly. 10. Carefully remove the mat and plastic wrap. 11. Repeat with remaining nori sheets and filling. 12. With a wet knife, cut each roll into bite-sized pieces. Serve with your favorite dipping sauce.

Per Serving: Calories 743; Total Fat 27.4g; Sodium 1215mg; Total Carbs 48.9g; Fiber 4.1g; Sugars 5.6g; Protein 81.1g

Salmon & Tuna Sushi Rolls

Preparation Time: 15 minutes | Servings: 5

Ingredients:

5 nori sheets
5 cups cooked and seasoned sushi rice (cooled)
2 ounces sushi-grade salmon, cut into 3-inch strips
2 ounces sushi-grade tuna, cut into 3-inch strips

1 cucumber, julienned
1 carrot, peeled and julienned
½ avocado, peeled, pitted and thinly sliced

Preparation:

1. Place 1 large-sized piece of plastic wrap onto a smooth surface. 2. Arrange 1 bamboo sushi mat over the plastic wrap. 3. Place 1 nori sheet on mat, shining-side-down, with the longer side of the nori facing you. 4. Place about 1 cup of rice over the nori, leaving a 1-inch border. 5. With your wet fingers, gently press the rice onto the nori in an even layer. 6. Arrange the salmon, tuna, cucumber, carrot and avocado across the center of the rice. 7. Carefully lift up the bottom edge of the sushi mat and then fold it over the filling into a roll. 8. With the sushi mat, squeeze the roll tightly. 9. Carefully remove the mat and plastic wrap. 10. Repeat with remaining nori sheets and filling. 11. With a wet knife, cut each roll into bite-sized pieces. Serve with your favorite dipping sauce.

Per Serving: Calories 525; Total Fat 8.4g; Sodium 425mg; Total Carbs 82.9g; Fiber 2.8g; Sugars 4.6g; Protein 16.9g

Tuna Mayonnaise Sushi Rolls

Preparation Time: 15 minutes | Servings: 4

Ingredients:

4 nori sheets
4 cups cooked and seasoned sushi rice (cooled)
⅔ cup canned tuna
1 tablespoon onion, finely cut up

1 tablespoon mayonnaise
1 teaspoon hot mustard
Pinch of salt

Preparation:

1. In a bowl, add the tuna, onion, mayonnaise, mustard and salt and blend to incorporate. 2. Place 1 large-sized piece of plastic wrap onto a smooth surface. 3. Arrange 1 bamboo sushi mat over the plastic wrap. 4. Place 1 nori sheet on mat, shining-side-down, with the longer side of the nori facing you. 5. Place about 1 cup of rice over the nori, leaving a 1-inch border. 6. With your wet fingers, gently press the rice onto the nori in an even layer. 7. Arrange the tuna mixture across the center of the rice. 8. Carefully lift up the bottom edge of the sushi mat and then fold it over the filling into a roll. 9. With the sushi mat, squeeze the roll tightly. 10. Carefully remove the mat and plastic wrap. 11. Repeat with remaining nori sheets and filling. 12. With a wet knife, cut each roll into bite-sized pieces. Serve with your favorite dipping sauce.

Per Serving: Calories 393; Total Fat 7.4g; Sodium 995mg; Total Carbs 60.9g; Fiber 0.1g; Sugars 9.6g; Protein 15.1g

Crab & Chives Sushi Rolls

Preparation Time: 15 minutes | Servings: 4

Ingredients:

6 ounces imitation crabmeat, cut up
3 tablespoons mayonnaise
2 tablespoons Sriracha
4 nori sheets

4 cups cooked and seasoned sushi rice (cooled)
1 cucumber, peeled and julienned
1 bunch fresh chives, cut up

Preparation:

1. In a medium-sized bowl, add crabmeat, mayonnaise and Sriracha and blend to incorporate. 2. Place 1 large-sized piece of plastic wrap onto a smooth surface. 3. Arrange 1 bamboo sushi mat over the plastic wrap. 4. Place 1 nori sheet on mat, shining-side-down, with the longer side of the nori facing you. 5. Place about 1 cup of rice over the nori, leaving a 1-inch border. 6. With your wet fingers, gently press the rice onto the nori in an even layer. 7. Arrange the crabmeat mixture, cucumber and chives across the center of the rice. 8. Carefully lift up the bottom edge of the sushi mat and then fold it over the filling into a roll. 9. With the sushi mat, squeeze the roll tightly. 10. Carefully remove the mat and plastic wrap. 11. Repeat with remaining nori sheets and filling. 12. With a wet knife, cut each roll into bite-sized pieces. Serve with your favorite dipping sauce.

Per Serving: Calories 480; Total Fat 23.4g; Sodium 125mg; Total Carbs 62.9g; Fiber 6.7g; Sugars 0.6g; Protein 13.1g

Salmon & Cucumber Sushi Rolls

Preparation Time: 15 minutes | Servings: 6

Ingredients:

6 nori sheets
6 cups cooked and seasoned sushi rice (cooled)
1 tablespoon prepared wasabi

½ pound sushi grade salmon, cut into ¼-inch thick strips
1 cucumber, peeled, seeded and cut into ¼-inch thick strips
3 scallions, cut into slices

Preparation:

1. Place 1 large-sized piece of plastic wrap onto a smooth surface. 2. Arrange 1 bamboo sushi mat over the plastic wrap. 3. Place 1 nori sheet on mat, shining-side-down, with the longer side of the nori facing you. 4. Place about 1 cup of rice over the nori, leaving a 1-inch border. 5. With your wet fingers, gently press the rice onto the nori in an even layer. 6. Place about ¼ teaspoon of wasabi on the centerline of rice. 7. Arrange the salmon, cucumber and scallion across the center of the rice. 8. Carefully lift up the bottom edge of the sushi mat and then fold it over the filling into a roll. 9. With the sushi mat, squeeze the roll tightly. 10. Carefully remove the mat and plastic wrap. 12. Repeat with remaining nori sheets and filling. 13. With a wet knife, cut each roll into bite-sized pieces. Serve with your favorite dipping sauce.

Per Serving: Calories 423; Total Fat 3.4g; Sodium 95mg; Total Carbs 69.9g; Fiber 2.1g; Sugars 0.6g; Protein 17.1g

Salmon & Cabbage Sushi Rolls

Preparation Time: 15 minutes | Servings: 4

Ingredients:

4 cups hot cooked sushi rice
¼ cup mirin
4 nori sheets
8 ounces cooked salmon, flaked

¼ of red cabbage head, finely shredded
1 carrot, peeled and cut into matchsticks
1 cucumber, cut into matchsticks

Preparation:

1. In a large-sized bowl, add the cooked rice and mirin and blend to incorporate thoroughly. Set aside to cool thoroughly. 2. Place 1 large-sized piece of plastic wrap onto a smooth surface. 3. Arrange 1 bamboo sushi mat over the plastic wrap. 4. Place 1 nori sheet on mat, shining-side-down, with the longer side of the nori facing you. 5. Place about 1 cup of rice over the nori, leaving a 1-inch border. 6. With your wet fingers, gently press the rice onto the nori in an even layer. 7. Arrange the salmon, cabbage, carrot and cucumber across the center of the rice. 8. Carefully lift up the bottom edge of the sushi mat and then fold it over the filling into a roll. 9. With the sushi mat, squeeze the roll tightly. 10. Carefully remove the mat and plastic wrap. 11. Repeat with remaining nori sheets and filling. 12. With a wet knife, cut each roll into bite-sized pieces. Serve with your favorite dipping sauce.

Per Serving: Calories 425; Total Fat 8.1g; Sodium 525mg; Total Carbs 56.2g; Fiber 5.3g; Sugars 7.6g; Protein 24.1g

Tuna & Wasabi Sushi Rolls

Preparation Time: 15 minutes | Servings: 4

Ingredients:

4 nori sheets
4 cups cooked and seasoned sushi rice (cooled)
½ pound sushi-grade fresh tuna, cut into ½-inch strips

Wasabi paste, as desired
2 tablespoons scallion, finely sliced
3 tablespoons sesame seeds, toasted

Preparation:

1. Place 1 large-sized piece of plastic wrap onto a smooth surface. 2. Arrange 1 bamboo sushi mat over the plastic wrap. 3. Place 1 nori sheet on mat, shining-side-down, with the longer side of the nori facing you. 4. Place about 1 cup of rice over the nori, leaving a 1-inch border. 5. With your wet fingers, gently press the rice onto the nori in an even layer. 6. Arrange the strips of tuna across the center of the rice. 7. Place a little of wasabi on the tuna and then sprinkle with scallion. 8. Carefully lift up the bottom edge of the sushi mat and then fold it over the filling into a roll. 9. With the sushi mat, squeeze the roll tightly. 10. Carefully remove the mat and plastic wrap. Sprinkle with the sesame seeds. 11. Repeat with remaining nori sheets and filling. 12. With a wet knife, cut each roll into bite-sized pieces. Serve with your favorite dipping sauce.

Per Serving: Calories 340; Total Fat 12.1g; Sodium 109mg; Total Carbs 38.7g; Fiber 1.1g; Sugars 1g; Protein 16.9g

Mango, Avocado & Cucumber Sushi Rolls

Preparation Time: 15 minutes | Servings: 2

Ingredients:

2 nori sheets
2 cups cooked and seasoned brown rice (cooled)
Sesame seeds, as desired

1 large avocado, sliced
1 cucumber, sliced
½ fresh mango, sliced

Preparation:

1. Place 1 large-sized piece of plastic wrap onto a smooth surface. 2. Arrange 1 bamboo sushi mat over the plastic wrap. 3. Place 1 nori sheet on mat, shining-side-down, with the longer side of the nori facing you. 4. Place about 1 cup of rice over the nori, leaving a 1-inch border. 5. With your wet fingers, gently press the rice onto the nori in an even layer. 6. Sprinkle the rice with sesame seeds. 7. Arrange the slices of avocado, mango and cucumber across the center of the rice. 8. Carefully lift up the bottom edge of the sushi mat and then fold it over the filling into a roll. 9. With the sushi mat, squeeze the roll tightly. 10. Carefully remove the mat and plastic wrap. 11. Repeat with remaining nori sheets and filling. 12. With a wet knife, cut each roll into bite-sized pieces. Serve with your favorite dipping sauce.

Per Serving: Calories 246; Total Fat 0.8g; Sodium 325mg; Total Carbs 55.9g; Fiber 2.5g; Sugars 1.6g; Protein 5.6g

Mango & Cream Cheese Sushi Rolls

Preparation Time: 15 minutes | Servings: 4

Ingredients:

4 nori sheets
4 cups cooked and seasoned sushi rice (cooled)
4 ounces cold cream cheese, cut into thin strips

1 mango, peeled, pitted and cut into thin strips
1 avocado, peeled, pitted and cut into thin strips

Preparation:

1. Place 1 large-sized piece of plastic wrap onto a smooth surface. 2. Arrange 1 bamboo sushi mat over the plastic wrap. 3. Place 1 nori sheet on mat, shining-side-down, with the longer side of the nori facing you. 4. Place about 1 cup of rice over the nori, leaving a 1-inch border. 5. With your wet fingers, gently press the rice onto the nori in an even layer. 6. Arrange the slices of cream cheese, mango and avocado across the center of the rice. 7. Carefully lift up the bottom edge of the sushi mat and then fold it over the filling into a roll. 8. With the sushi mat, squeeze the roll tightly. 9. Carefully remove the mat and plastic wrap. 10. Repeat with remaining nori sheets and filling. 11. With a wet knife, cut each roll into bite-sized pieces. Serve with your favorite dipping sauce.

Per Serving: Calories 259; Total Fat 8.4g; Sodium 425mg; Total Carbs 29.2g; Fiber 6.1g; Sugars 12.9g; Protein 3.8g

Eggs, Avocado & Veggie Sushi Rolls

Preparation Time: 15 minutes | Cooking Time: 2 minutes | Servings: 4

Ingredients:

2 large eggs
1 teaspoon water
Salt, as desired
1 teaspoon vegetable oil
4 nori sheets

4 cups cooked and seasoned sushi rice (cooled)
1 carrot, cut into matchsticks
1 small yellow bell pepper, stemmed, seeded and cut into matchsticks
½ of avocado, peeled, pitted and thinly sliced

Preparation:

1. In a small-sized bowl, add the eggs, water and a pinch of salt and whisk thoroughly. 2. In a non-stick wok, heat oil over medium heat. 3. Add the egg and spread into a thin circular layer. 4. Cook for around 1 minute. 5. Carefully flip the egg and cook for around 20-30 seconds. 6. Transfer the cooked egg onto a cutting board and let it cool slightly. 7. Cut the egg into thin slices and set aside. 8. Place 1 large-sized piece of plastic wrap onto a smooth surface. 9. Arrange 1 bamboo sushi mat over the plastic wrap. 10. Place 1 nori sheet on mat, shining-side-down, with the longer side of the nori facing you. 11. Place about 1 cup of rice over the nori, leaving a 1-inch border. 12. With your wet fingers, gently press the rice onto the nori in an even layer. 13. Arrange the carrot, bell pepper, avocado and egg slices across the center of the rice. 14. Carefully lift up the bottom edge of the sushi mat and then fold it over the filling into a roll. 15. With the sushi mat, squeeze the roll tightly. 16. Carefully remove the mat and plastic wrap. 17. Repeat with remaining nori sheets and filling. 18. With a wet knife, cut each roll into bite-sized pieces. Serve with your favorite dipping sauce.

Per Serving: Calories 343; Total Fat 4.4g; Sodium 629mg; Total Carbs 66.9g; Fiber 1.1g; Sugars 3.6g; Protein 9.9g

Crab & Mango Sushi Rolls

Preparation Time: 15 minutes | Servings: 5

Ingredients:

¼ cup mayonnaise
1 tablespoon brown sugar
1 tablespoon fresh lemon juice
1-pound lump crabmeat, drained and patted dry
5 cups cooked sushi rice

¼ cup seasoned rice vinegar
5 nori sheets
1 large mango, peeled, pitted and thinly sliced
1 large avocado, peeled, pitted and thinly sliced
1 small bell pepper, seeded and thinly sliced

Preparation:

1. In a medium-sized bowl, mix together the mayonnaise, sugar and lemon juice. 2. Add crabmeat and blend to incorporate. 3. In another bowl, mix together rice and vinegar. 4. Place 1 large-sized piece of plastic wrap onto a smooth surface. 5. Arrange 1 bamboo sushi mat over the plastic wrap. 6. Place 1 nori sheet on mat, shining-side-down, with the longer side of the nori facing you. 7. Place about 1 cup of rice over the nori, leaving a 1-inch border. 8. With your wet fingers, gently press the rice onto the nori in an even layer. 9. Arrange the crab mixture, mango, avocado and bell pepper across the center of the rice. 10. Carefully lift up the bottom edge of the sushi mat and then fold it over the filling into a roll. 11. With the sushi mat, squeeze the roll tightly. 12. Carefully remove the mat and plastic wrap. 13. Repeat with remaining nori sheet and filling. 14. With a wet knife, cut each roll into bite-sized pieces. Serve with your favorite dipping sauce.

Per Serving: Calories 638; Total fat 24.4g; Sodium 6mg; Total Carbs 70.2g; Fiber 7.4g; Sugars 10.6g; Protein 37.4g

Corned Beef & Avocado Sushi Rolls

Preparation Time: 15 minutes | Servings: 2

Ingredients:

2 nori sheets
2 cups cooked and seasoned sushi rice (cooled)
6 thin corned beef slices

½ avocado, peeled, pitted and sliced
¼ cucumber, cut into thin strips

Preparation:

1. Place 1 large-sized piece of plastic wrap onto a smooth surface. 2. Arrange 1 bamboo sushi mat over the plastic wrap. 3. Place 1 nori sheet on mat, shining-side-down, with the longer side of the nori facing you. 4. Place about 1 cup of rice over the nori, leaving a 1-inch border. 5. With your wet fingers, gently press the rice onto the nori in an even layer. 6. Arrange the corned beef, avocado and cucumber across the center of the rice. 7. Carefully lift up the bottom edge of the sushi mat and then fold it over the filling into a roll. 8. With the sushi mat, squeeze the roll tightly. 9. Carefully remove the mat and plastic wrap. 10. Repeat with remaining nori sheets and filling. 11. With a wet knife, cut each roll into bite-sized pieces. Serve with your favorite dipping sauce.

Per Serving: Calories 363; Total Fat 8.9g; Sodium 325mg; Total Carbs 65.9g; Fiber 4.9g; Sugars 4.6g; Protein 13.1g

Beef & Bell Pepper Sushi Rolls

Preparation Time: 15 minutes | Servings: 4

Ingredients:

4 nori sheets
4 cups cooked and seasoned sushi rice (cooled)
6 ounces cooked beef, cut into thin strips

1 cup bell pepper, seeded and cut into thin strips
¼ cup Asian-style dressing

Preparation:

1. Place 1 large-sized piece of plastic wrap onto a smooth surface. 2. Arrange 1 bamboo sushi mat over the plastic wrap. 3. Place 1 nori sheet on mat, shining-side-down, with the longer side of the nori facing you. 4. Place about 1 cup of rice over the nori, leaving a 1-inch border. 5. With your wet fingers, gently press the rice onto the nori in an even layer. 6. Arrange the beef and bell pepper across the center of the rice. Drizzle the top with dressing. 7. Carefully lift up the bottom edge of the sushi mat and then fold it over the filling into a roll. 8. With the sushi mat, squeeze the roll tightly. 9. Carefully remove the mat and plastic wrap. 10. Repeat with remaining nori sheets and filling. 11. With a wet knife, cut each roll into bite-sized pieces. Serve with your favorite dipping sauce.

Per Serving: Calories 248; Total Fat 5.4g; Sodium 250mg; Total Carbs 39.9g; Fiber 1.6g; Sugars 2.6g; Protein 19.1g

Snapper Sushi Rolls

Preparation Time: 15 minutes | Servings: 4

Ingredients:

4 nori sheets
4 cups cooked and seasoned sushi rice (cooled)
1 (8-ounce) boneless red snapper fillet, cut into ½-inch strips
2 tablespoons mayonnaise

2 tablespoons Sriracha
1 cucumber, peeled and sliced lengthwise into ½-inch wide strips
1 avocado, peeled, pitted and cut into ½-inch pieces

Preparation:

1. Refrigerate the snapper strips before using. 2. In a small-sized bowl, add the mayonnaise and Sriracha and whisk to incorporate. 3. Place 1 large-sized piece of plastic wrap onto a smooth surface. 4. Arrange 1 bamboo sushi mat over the plastic wrap. 5. Place 1 nori sheet on mat, shining-side-down, with the longer side of the nori facing you. 6. Place about 1 cup of rice over the nori, leaving a 1-inch border. 7. With your wet fingers, gently press the rice onto the nori in an even layer. 8. Place about 2 teaspoons of the Sriracha mayonnaise across the center of the nori sheet. 9. Arrange the strips of snapper, cucumber and avocado across the center of the rice. 10. Carefully lift up the bottom edge of the sushi mat and then fold it over the filling into a roll. 11. With the sushi mat, squeeze the roll tightly. 12. Carefully remove the mat and plastic wrap. 13. Repeat with remaining nori sheets and filling. 14. With a wet knife, cut each roll into bite-sized pieces. Serve with your favorite dipping sauce.

Per Serving: Calories 430; Total Fat 9.4g; Sodium 125mg; Total Carbs 58.9g; Fiber 2.1g; Sugars 4.6g; Protein 22.1g

Shrimp & Seaweed Caviar Sushi Rolls

Preparation Time: 15 minutes | Servings: 4

Ingredients:

2 nori sheets
2 cups cooked and seasoned sushi rice (cooled)
4 tablespoons seaweed caviar, divided

4 cooked jumbo shrimp
1 cucumber, seeded and julienned
½ avocado, peeled, pitted and sliced

Preparation:

1. Place 1 large-sized piece of plastic wrap onto a smooth surface. 2. Arrange 1 bamboo sushi mat over the plastic wrap. 3. Place 1 nori sheet on mat, shining-side-down, with the longer side of the nori facing you. 4. Place about 1 cup of rice over the nori, leaving a 1-inch border. 5. With your wet fingers, gently press the rice onto the nori in an even layer. 6. Place seaweed caviar over the rice. 7. Arrange the shrimp, cucumber and avocado across the center of the rice. 8. Carefully lift up the bottom edge of the sushi mat and then fold it over the filling into a roll. 9. With the sushi mat, squeeze the roll tightly. 10. Carefully remove the mat and plastic wrap. 11. Repeat with remaining nori sheets and filling. 12. With a wet knife, cut each roll into bite-sized pieces. Serve with your favorite dipping sauce.

Per Serving: Calories 468; Total Fat 18.4g; Sodium 925mg; Total Carbs 60.9g; Fiber 3.1g; Sugars 3.6g; Protein 17.6g

Lemony Crab Sushi Rolls

Preparation Time: 15 minutes | Servings: 4

Ingredients:

6 ounces cooked crabmeat, picked through for bits of shell or cartilage
1 tablespoon fresh lemon juice
4 nori sheets

4 cups cooked and seasoned sushi rice (cooled)
2 teaspoons sesame seeds, toasted
1 medium avocado, peeled, pitted and cut into ⅛-inch-thick slices
1 cucumber, seeded and cut into thin sticks

Preparation:

1. Gently squeeze the crabmeat to drain out any excess liquid. 2. In a medium-sized bowl, add the crabmeat and lemon juice and blend thoroughly. 3. Place 1 large-sized piece of plastic wrap onto a smooth surface. 4. Arrange 1 bamboo sushi mat over the plastic wrap. 5. Place 1 nori sheet on mat, shining-side-down, with the longer side of the nori facing you. 6. Place about 1 cup of rice over the nori, leaving a 1-inch border. 7. With your wet fingers, gently press the rice onto the nori in an even layer. 8. Sprinkle the rice with sesame seeds. 9. Arrange the crabmeat, avocado and cucumber across the center of the rice. 10. Carefully lift up the bottom edge of the sushi mat and then fold it over the filling into a roll. 11. With the sushi mat, squeeze the roll tightly. 12. Carefully remove the mat and plastic wrap. 13. Repeat with remaining nori sheets and filling. 14. With a wet knife, cut each roll into bite-sized pieces. Serve with your favorite dipping sauce.

Per Serving: Calories 243; Total Fat 12.4g; Sodium 825mg; Total Carbs 32.9g; Fiber 4.1g; Sugars 1.6g; Protein 10.1g

Tuna & Cucumber Sushi Rolls

Preparation Time: 15 minutes | Servings: 4

Ingredients:

4 nori sheets
4 cups cooked and seasoned sushi rice (cooled)
1 tablespoon sesame seeds, toasted
1 tablespoon wasabi horseradish, finely grated

2 teaspoons spicy chili oil
6 ounces sushi-grade tuna fillet, cut into ¼-inch thick slices
1 cucumber, peeled, seeded and cut into thin strips

Preparation:

1. Place 1 large-sized piece of plastic wrap onto a smooth surface. 2. Arrange 1 bamboo sushi mat over the plastic wrap. 3. Place 1 nori sheet on mat, shining-side-down, with the longer side of the nori facing you. 4. Place about 1 cup of rice over the nori, leaving a 1-inch border. 5. With your wet fingers, gently press the rice onto the nori in an even layer. 6. Sprinkle the rice with sesame seeds. 7. Place a thin line of wasabi across the center of rice and drizzle with chili oil. 8. Arrange the tuna strips and cucumber across the center of the rice. 9. Carefully lift up the bottom edge of the sushi mat and then fold it over the filling into a roll. 10. With the sushi mat, squeeze the roll tightly. 11. Carefully remove the mat and plastic wrap. 12. Repeat with remaining nori sheets and filling. 13. With a wet knife, cut each roll into bite-sized pieces. Serve with your favorite dipping sauce.

Per Serving: Calories 723; Total Fat 5.4g; Sodium 125mg; Total Carbs 82.9g; Fiber 1.1g; Sugars 2.6g; Protein 25.1g

Tempura Shrimp & Crab Sushi Rolls

Preparation Time: 15 minutes | Cooking Time: 12 minutes | Servings: 2

Ingredients:

Non-stick baking spray
2 nori sheets
2 cups cooked and seasoned sushi rice (cooled)

8 frozen tempura shrimp
2 imitation crabmeat sticks, cut into ¼-inch pieces
1 cucumber, peeled, seeded and cut into ¼-inch strips

Preparation:

1. For preheating: set your oven at 400°F. 2. Grease a baking sheet with baking spray. 3. Arrange the shrimp tempura onto the baking sheet. 4. Bake for around 6 minutes per side. 5. Remove from oven and cut the tails of the shrimp tempura. 6. Place 1 large-sized piece of plastic wrap onto a smooth surface. 7. Arrange 1 bamboo sushi mat over the plastic wrap. 8. Place 1 nori sheet on mat, shining-side-down, with the longer side of the nori facing you. 9. Place about 1 cup of rice over the nori, leaving a 1-inch border. 10. With your wet fingers, gently press the rice onto the nori in an even layer. 11. Arrange the crabmeat, cucumber and shrimp across the center of the rice. 12. Carefully lift up the bottom edge of the sushi mat and then fold it over the filling into a roll. 13. With the sushi mat, squeeze the roll tightly. 14. Carefully remove the mat and plastic wrap. 15. Repeat with remaining nori sheet and filling. 16. With a wet knife, cut each roll into bite-sized pieces. Serve with your favorite dipping sauce.

Per Serving: Calories 243; Total Fat 15.4g; Sodium 975mg; Total Carbs 45.9g; Fiber 8.1g; Sugars 10.6g; Protein 16.1g

Seafood & Veggies Sushi Rolls

Preparation Time: 20 minutes | Servings: 10

Ingredients:

10 nori sheets
10 cups cooked and seasoned sushi rice (cooled)
10 blanched asparagus spears
1 red pepper, julienned
1 cucumber, seeded and sliced thinly

1 avocado, peeled, pitted and sliced thin
½ pound crabmeat
1-pound raw tuna
1 pound smoked salmon

Preparation:

1. Place 1 large-sized piece of plastic wrap onto a smooth surface. 2. Arrange 1 bamboo sushi mat over the plastic wrap. 3. Place 1 nori sheet on mat, shining-side-down, with the longer side of the nori facing you. 4. Place about 1 cup of rice over the nori, leaving a 1-inch border. 5. With your wet fingers, gently press the rice onto the nori in an even layer. 6. Arrange the vegetables and seafood across the center of the rice. 7. Carefully lift up the bottom edge of the sushi mat and then fold it over the filling into a roll. 8. With the sushi mat, squeeze the roll tightly. 9. Carefully remove the mat and plastic wrap. 10. Repeat with remaining nori sheets and filling. 11. With a wet knife, cut each roll into bite-sized pieces. Serve with your favorite dipping sauce.

Per Serving: Calories 442; Total Fat 22.4g; Sodium 696mg; Total Carbs 69.9g; Fiber 3.8g; Sugars 7.1g; Protein 19.9g

Smoked Trout Sushi Rolls

Preparation Time: 15 minutes | Servings: 2

Ingredients:

2 cups cooked sushi rice
¼ cup rice vinegar
1 tablespoon white sugar
½ teaspoon salt

2 nori sheets
2 tablespoons cream cheese, softened
4 ounces smoked trout, flaked
4-6 thin cucumber slices

Preparation:

1. In a bowl, add the rice, vinegar, sugar and salt and blend to incorporate. Set aside to cool. 2. Place 1 large-sized piece of plastic wrap onto a smooth surface. 3. Arrange 1 bamboo sushi mat over the plastic wrap. 4. Place 1 nori sheet on mat, shining-side-down, with the longer side of the nori facing you. 5. Place 1 cup of rice over the nori, leaving a 1-inch border. 6. With your wet fingers, gently press the rice onto the nori in an even layer. 7. Spread the cream cheese across center of rice. 8. Arrange the trout and cucumber slices across the center of the rice. 9. Carefully lift up the bottom edge of the sushi mat and then fold it over the filling into a roll. 10. With the sushi mat, squeeze the roll tightly. 11. Carefully remove the mat and plastic wrap. 12. Repeat with remaining nori sheet and filling. 13. With a wet knife, cut each roll into bite-sized pieces. Serve with your favorite dipping sauce.

Per Serving: Calories 319; Total fat 12.2g; Sodium 173mg; Total Carbs 36g; Fiber 3.8g; Sugars 1.8g; Protein 16.6g

Gingered Crab Sushi Rolls

Preparation Time: 15 minutes | Servings: 2

Ingredients:

2 nori sheets
¼ cucumber, peeled and thinly sliced
2 (3-ounce) imitation crabmeat fillets, cut into small pieces

1½ ounces cream cheese, sliced
2 cups cooked and seasoned sushi rice (cooled)
1 (1-inch) piece fresh ginger, finely cut up

Preparation:

1. Place 1 large-sized piece of plastic wrap onto a smooth surface. 2. Arrange 1 bamboo sushi mat over the plastic wrap. 3. Place 1 nori sheet on mat, shining-side-down, with the longer side of the nori facing you. 4. Place about 1 cup of rice over the nori, leaving a 1-inch border. 5. With your wet fingers, gently press the rice onto the nori in an even layer. 6. Arrange the cucumber, crabmeat and cream cheese across the center of the rice. 7. Sprinkle with ginger evenly. 8. Carefully lift up the bottom edge of the sushi mat and then fold it over the filling into a roll. 9. With the sushi mat, squeeze the roll tightly. 10. Carefully remove the mat and plastic wrap. 11. Repeat with remaining nori sheet and filling. 12. With a wet knife, cut each roll into bite-sized pieces. Serve with your favorite dipping sauce.

Per Serving: Calories 445; Total fat 9.4g; Sodium 1501mg; Total Carbs 78.9g; Fiber 2.1g; Sugars 13.6g; Protein 15.4g

Wasabi Crab Sushi Rolls

Preparation Time: 15 minutes | Servings: 3

Ingredients:

¼ cup mayonnaise
1 tablespoon chile sauce
1½ teaspoons Japanese seven spice
1 teaspoon prepared wasabi
1 teaspoon paprika

1 teaspoon red chili powder
3 (3-ounce) imitation crabmeat fillets, cut into 1½-inch pieces
3 nori sheets
3 cups cooked and seasoned sushi rice (cooled)
2 avocados, peeled, pitted and thinly sliced

Preparation:

1. In a small-sized bowl, add mayonnaise, chile sauce, Japanese seven spice, wasabi, paprika and chili powder and blend to incorporate. 2. Gently fold in the crabmeat. 3. Place 1 large-sized piece of plastic wrap onto a smooth surface. 4. Arrange 1 bamboo sushi mat over the plastic wrap. 5. Place 1 nori sheet on mat, shining-side-down, with the longer side of the nori facing you. 6. Place about 1 cup of rice over the nori, leaving a 1-inch border. 7. With your wet fingers, gently press the rice onto the nori in an even layer. 8. Arrange the crabmeat and slices of avocado across the center of the rice. 9. Carefully lift up the bottom edge of the sushi mat and then fold it over the filling into a roll. 10. With the sushi mat, squeeze the roll tightly. 11. Carefully remove the mat and plastic wrap. 12. Repeat with remaining nori sheet and filling. 13. With a wet knife, cut each roll into bite-sized pieces. Serve with your favorite dipping sauce.

Per Serving: Calories 340; Total fat 16.9g; Sodium 6mg; Total Carbs 41.8g; Fiber 5.3g; Sugars 3.7g; Protein 11.2g

Tomato & Avocado Sushi Rolls

Preparation Time: 15 minutes | Cooking Time: 2 minutes | Servings: 3

Ingredients:

2 large tomatoes
1½ tablespoons soy sauce
½ tablespoons kelp powder
½ tablespoons Sriracha
½ tablespoons sesame oil

½ teaspoons fresh ginger, finely cut up
3 nori sheets
½ small cucumber, peeled and cut into thin matchsticks
½ avocado, peeled, pitted and cut into thin matchsticks

Preparation:

1. With a knife, pierce the tomatoes. 2. In a small-sized saucepan of boiling water, add the tomatoes and cook for around 1-2 minutes. 3. With a slotted spoon, transfer the tomatoes into a large-sized bowl of ice water. 4. Drain the tomatoes and remove the peel. 5. Then chop the tomatoes. 6. In a container, add the soy sauce, kelp powder, Sriracha, sesame oil and ginger and blend to incorporate thoroughly. 7. Add the tomato pieces and gently blend to incorporate. 8. Place 1 large-sized piece of plastic wrap onto a smooth surface. 9. Arrange 1 bamboo sushi mat over the plastic wrap. 10. Place 1 nori sheet on mat, shining-side-down, with the longer side of the nori facing you. 11. Place about 1 cup of rice over the nori, leaving a 1-inch border. 12. With your wet fingers, gently press the rice onto the nori in an even layer. 13. Arrange the tomato mixture, cucumber and avocado across the center of the rice. 14. Carefully lift up the bottom edge of the sushi mat and then fold it over the filling into a roll. 15. With the sushi mat, squeeze the roll tightly. 16. Carefully remove the mat and plastic wrap. 17. Repeat with remaining nori sheets and filling. 18. With a wet knife, cut each roll into bite-sized pieces. Serve with your favorite dipping sauce.

Per Serving: Calories 264; Total fat 6.9g; Sodium 776mg; Total Carbs 45.9g; Fiber 3.6g; Sugars 6.1g; Protein 6.2g

Asparagus, Mushroom & Avocado Sushi Rolls

Preparation Time: 20 minutes | Cooking Time: 10 minutes | Servings: 4

Ingredients:

½ cup water
1 (2-inch) piece fresh ginger, peeled and thinly sliced
¼ cup brown rice vinegar
1 tablespoon raw honey
¼ teaspoon salt
5 nori sheets

5 cups cooked brown rice
¼ cup sesame seeds
2 tablespoons nutritional yeast
4 asparagus spears, trimmed
2 shiitake mushrooms, thinly sliced
½ avocado, peeled, pitted and thinly sliced

Preparation:

1. For pickled ginger: in a small-sized saucepan, add water and bring to a boil. 2. Remove the saucepan of water from heat and stir in ginger. 3. Set aside for around 5 minutes. 4. In a small-sized bowl, add vinegar, honey and salt and whisk to incorporate thoroughly. 5. With a slotted spoon, transfer the ginger slices into the bowl of honey mixture. 6. Add about ¼ cup of ginger water and stir to incorporate thoroughly. 7. Set aside for around 30 minutes. 8. Meanwhile, in a medium-sized saucepan of boiling water, add the asparagus spears and mushrooms; cook for around 3-4 minutes. 9. Drain the water and immediately plunge the asparagus spears into a bowl of ice water. 10. After cooling, drain the asparagus spears and with paper towels pat dry them. 11. Drain the ginger slices. 12. In a large-sized bowl, add rice, ginger slices, sesame seeds and nutritional yeast and blend to incorporate thoroughly. 13. Place 1 large-sized piece of plastic wrap onto a smooth surface. 14. Arrange 1 bamboo sushi mat over the plastic wrap. 15. Place 1 nori sheet on mat, shining-side-down, with the longer side of the nori facing you. 16. Place 1 cup of rice over the nori, leaving a 1-inch border. 17. With your wet fingers, gently press the rice onto the nori in an even layer. 18. Arrange the slices of mushroom and avocado across the center of the rice. 19. Carefully lift up the bottom edge of the sushi mat and then fold it over the filling into a roll. 20. With the sushi mat, squeeze the roll tightly. 21. Carefully remove the mat and plastic wrap. 22. Repeat with remaining nori sheets and filling. 23. With a wet knife, cut each roll into bite-sized pieces. Serve with your favorite dipping sauce.

Per Serving: Calories 336; Total fat 9.3g; Sodium 136mg; Total Carbs 55.1g; Fiber 5.6g; Sugars 4.4g; Protein 8.9g

Beef, Tuna & Egg Sushi Rolls

Preparation Time: 20 minutes | Cooking Time: 20 minutes | Servings: 6

Ingredients:

2 Swiss chard leaves
2 eggs, well whisked
2 tablespoons soy sauce, divided
3 tablespoons water
1 onion, cut up
1 tablespoon vegetable oil

¾ pound ground beef
1 (5-ounce) can tuna, drained
6 nori sheets
6 cups cooked and seasoned sushi rice
1 carrot, peeled and julienned
1 cucumber, julienned

Preparation:

1. In a medium-sized saucepan of boiling water, cook the chard leaves for around 2-3 minutes or until tender. 2. Drain the chard leaves well and set aside to cool. 3. In a medium-sized wok, heat 1 tablespoon of vegetable oil over medium-high heat and cook the onion for around 3-4 minutes. 4. Add in garlic and cook for 1 minute. 5. Stir in the beef and 1 tablespoon of soy sauce and cook for around 8-10 minutes. 6. Remove the wok of beef from heat and drain the excess grease. Set aside to cool thoroughly. 7. In a bowl, add the eggs, water and remaining soy sauce and beat to incorporate thoroughly. 8. In a medium-sized frying pan, heat remaining vegetable oil over medium heat. 9. Add eggs and cook for around 3-4 minutes or until set thoroughly, flipping once halfway through. 10. Remove the cooked eggs from heat and place onto a cutting board. 11. Cut the cooked egg into strips and set aside. 12. After cooling, cut the chard leaves into thin strips. 13. Place 1 large-sized piece of plastic wrap onto a smooth surface. 14. Arrange 1 bamboo sushi mat over the plastic wrap. 15. Place 1 nori sheet on mat, shining-side-down, with the longer side of the nori facing you. 16. Place about 1 cup of rice over the nori, leaving a 1-inch border. 17. With your wet fingers, gently press the rice onto the nori in an even layer. 18. Arrange the cooked beef, egg strips, chard strips, carrot and cucumber across the center of the rice. 19. Carefully lift up the bottom edge of the sushi mat and then fold it over the filling into a roll. 20. With the sushi mat, squeeze the roll tightly. 21. Carefully remove the mat and plastic wrap. 22. Repeat with remaining nori sheet and filling. 23. With a wet knife, cut each roll into bite-sized pieces. Serve with your favorite dipping sauce.

Per Serving: Calories 484; Total fat 19.4g; Sodium 496mg; Total Carbs 58.9g; Fiber 3.6g; Sugars 3.6g; Protein 24.5g

Sweet Chili Chicken Sushi Rolls

Preparation Time: 15 minutes | Cooking Time: 5 minutes | Servings: 4

Ingredients:

4 cups hot cooked sushi rice
¼ cup mirin seasoning
½ pound chicken tenderloins, cut into thin strips
¼ cup sweet chili sauce, divided
2 teaspoons olive oil

2 tablespoons mayonnaise
4 nori sheets
½ of cucumber, cut into thin strips
½ of medium avocado, peeled, pitted and thinly sliced
1 cup lettuce leaves, torn

Preparation:

1. In a large-sized bowl, add hot rice and mirin seasoning and blend to incorporate. 2. Set aside at room temperature to cool thoroughly. 3. In a small-sized bowl, add the chicken strips and half of sweet chili sauce and toss to incorporate thoroughly. 4. In a small-sized frying pan, heat olive oil over medium-high heat and sear the chicken strips for around 5 minutes. 5. Meanwhile, in a small-sized bowl, mix together mayonnaise and remaining sweet chili sauce. 6. Place 1 large-sized piece of plastic wrap onto a smooth surface. 7. Arrange 1 bamboo sushi mat over the plastic wrap. 8. Place 1 nori sheet on mat, shining-side-down, with the longer side of the nori facing you. 9. Place about 1 cup of rice over the nori, leaving a 1-inch border. 10. With your wet fingers, gently press the rice onto the nori in an even layer. 11. Spread the mayonnaise mixture across center of rice. 12. Arrange the slices of chicken, avocado, cucumber and lettuce across the center of the rice. 13. Carefully lift up the bottom edge of the sushi mat and then fold it over the filling into a roll. 14. With the sushi mat, squeeze the roll tightly. 15. Carefully remove the mat and plastic wrap. 16. Repeat with remaining nori sheets and filling. 17. With a wet knife, cut each roll into bite-sized pieces. Serve with your favorite dipping sauce.

Per Serving: Calories 396; Total fat 11.6g; Sodium 316mg; Total Carbs 53.2g; Fiber 2.6g; Sugars 7.6g; Protein 17.2g

Sweet Potato & Avocado Sushi Rolls

Preparation Time: 20 minutes | Cooking Time: 20 minutes | Servings: 4

Ingredients:

1 medium sweet potato, peeled and cut into 2-ish inch strips
⅔ cups almond milk
2 tablespoons flaxseed meal
⅓ cup cornstarch
1 teaspoon paprika
1 teaspoon onion powder

1 teaspoon garlic powder
1 teaspoon salt
Non-stick baking spray
4 nori sheets
4 cups cooked sushi rice
1 avocado, peeled, pitted and cut into strips

Preparation:

1. For preheating: set your oven at 425°F. 2. Line a large-sized baking sheet with parchment paper. 3. In a shallow bowl, add the almond milk and flaxseed meal and blend thoroughly. Set aside for 5 minutes. 4. In a separate shallow bowl, add the cornstarch, spices and salt and blend thoroughly. 5. Dip each sweet potato strip into milk mixture and then coat with cornstarch mixture. 6. Arrange the sweet potato strips onto the prepared baking sheet. 7. Spray the top of the sweet potato strips with baking spray. 8. Bake for around 10 minutes. 9. Flip the sweet potato strips and spray with baking spray. 10. Bake for around 10 minutes. 11. Remove from oven and set aside to cool. 12. Place 1 large-sized piece of plastic wrap onto a smooth surface. 13. Arrange 1 bamboo sushi mat over the plastic wrap. 14. Place 1 nori sheet on mat, shining-side-down, with the longer side of the nori facing you. 15. Place 1 cup of rice over the nori, leaving a 1-inch border. 16. With your wet fingers, gently press the rice onto the nori in an even layer. 17. Arrange the sweet potato strips and avocado across the center of the rice. 18. Carefully lift up the bottom edge of the sushi mat and then fold it over the filling into a roll. 19. With the sushi mat, squeeze the roll tightly. 20. Carefully remove the mat and plastic wrap. 21. Repeat with remaining nori sheets and filling. 22. With a wet knife, cut each roll into bite-sized pieces. Serve with your favorite dipping sauce.

Per Serving: Calories 289; Total fat 7.4g; Sodium 716mg; Total Carbs 48.9g; Fiber 2.6g; Sugars 2.2g; Protein 5.2g

Savory Veggies & Eggs Sushi Rolls

Preparation Time: 15 minutes | Cooking Time: 9 minutes | Servings: 4

Ingredients:

4 cups hot cooked short-grain white rice
2 teaspoons sesame oil
Salt, as desired
1 medium carrot, peeled and julienned
Salt, as desired

1 medium cucumber, seeded and julienned
2 large eggs, whisked
4 nori sheets
10 ounces cooked spinach
½ cup pickled radishes, drained and julienned

Preparation:

1. In a bowl, add the rice, sesame oil and salt and blend to incorporate. Set aside to cool. 2. Heat a non-stick wok over medium heat and stir-fry the carrot with a pinch of salt for around 2-3 minutes. 3. Transfer the carrot onto a plate. 4. In the same wok, add the cucumber with a pinch of salt and stir-fry for around 2-3 minutes. 5. Transfer the cucumber onto the plate with carrot. 6. In a small-sized bowl, whisk the eggs. 7. Heat a greased, small-sized frying pan over medium heat. 8. Add eggs and cook for around 2-3 minutes or until set thoroughly, flipping once halfway through. 9. Remove the cooked eggs from heat and place onto a cutting board. 10. Cut the cooked egg into strips and set aside. 11. Place 1 large-sized piece of plastic wrap onto a smooth surface. 12. Arrange 1 bamboo sushi mat over the plastic wrap. 13. Place 1 nori sheet on mat, shining-side-down, with the longer side of the nori facing you. 14. Place about 1 cup of rice over the nori, leaving a 1-inch border. 15. With your wet fingers, gently press the rice onto the nori in an even layer. 16. Arrange the cooked vegetables, egg strips, spinach and radishes across the center of the rice. 17. Carefully lift up the bottom edge of the sushi mat and then fold it over the filling into a roll. 18. With the sushi mat, squeeze the roll tightly. 19. Carefully remove the mat and plastic wrap. 20. Repeat with remaining nori sheet and filling. 21. With a wet knife, cut each roll into bite-sized pieces. Serve with your favorite dipping sauce.

Per Serving: Calories 184; Total fat 6.4g; Sodium 796mg; Total Carbs 28.9g; Fiber 2.9g; Sugars 3.2g; Protein 8.1g

Sweet Potato, Beet & Avocado Sushi Rolls

Preparation Time: 20 minutes | Cooking Time: 25 minutes | Servings: 4

Ingredients:

1 tablespoon maple syrup
1 tablespoon vegetable oil
1 teaspoon sesame oil
½ tablespoon soy sauce
1 large sweet potato, peeled and cut into ½-inch thick strips lengthwise
1 beet, peeled and cut into ¼-inch thick strips lengthwise

Salt and ground black pepper, as desired
1 tablespoon olive oil
3 teaspoons sesame seeds
4 nori sheets
4 cups cooked and seasoned sushi rice (cooled)
1 avocado, peeled, pitted and thinly sliced

Preparation:

1. For preheating: set your oven at 400ºF. 2. Line a baking sheet with parchment paper. 3. For the roasted veggies: In a large-sized bowl, add the maple syrup, vegetable oil, sesame oil and soy sauce and blend to incorporate thoroughly. 4. Add the sweet potato and beet strips and coat with the mixture evenly. 5. Arrange the sweet potato and beet strips onto the prepared baking sheet in a single layer. 6. Sprinkle the veggies with salt and pepper. 7. Bake for around 20-25 minutes, flipping once halfway through. 8. Remove the baking sheet from oven and set aside to cool. 9. Place 1 large-sized piece of plastic wrap onto a smooth surface. 10. Arrange 1 bamboo sushi mat over the plastic wrap. 11. Place 1 nori sheet on mat, shining-side-down, with the longer side of the nori facing you. 12. Place about 1 cup of rice over the nori, leaving a 1-inch border. 13. With your wet fingers, gently press the rice onto the nori in an even layer. 14. Arrange the sweet potato, beet and avocado across the center of the rice. 15. Carefully lift up the bottom edge of the sushi mat and then fold it over the filling into a roll. 16. With the sushi mat, squeeze the roll tightly. 17. Carefully remove the mat and plastic wrap. 18. Repeat with remaining nori sheets and filling. 19. With a wet knife, cut each roll into bite-sized pieces. Serve with your favorite dipping sauce.

Per Serving: Calories 321; Total fat 10.4g; Sodium 1496mg; Total Carbs 58.9g; Fiber 5.6g; Sugars 8.6g; Protein 6.3g

Mango, Kimchi & Bell Pepper Sushi Rolls

Preparation Time: 15 minutes | Servings: 4

Ingredients:

2 cups cooked brown rice (hot)
1 tablespoon brown rice vinegar
1 teaspoon mirin
1 teaspoon maple syrup
½ teaspoon salt

2 nori sheets
½ of mango, peeled, pitted and sliced into thin strips
¼ of bell pepper, seeded and thinly sliced into strips
½ of avocado, peeled, pitted and sliced into thin strips
½ cup kimchi

Preparation:

1. In a large-sized bowl, add the cooked rice, vinegar, mirin, maple syrup and salt and blend to incorporate thoroughly. 2. Set aside to cool thoroughly. 3. Place 1 large-sized piece of plastic wrap onto a smooth surface. 4. Arrange 1 bamboo sushi mat over the plastic wrap. 5. Place 1 nori sheet on mat, shining-side-down, with the longer side of the nori facing you. 6. Place 1 cup of rice over the nori, leaving a 1-inch border. 7. With your wet fingers, gently press the rice onto the nori in an even layer. 8. Arrange the mango, avocado, bell pepper and kimchi across the center of the rice. 9. Carefully lift up the bottom edge of the sushi mat and then fold it over the filling into a roll. 10. With the sushi mat, squeeze the roll tightly. 11. Carefully remove the mat and plastic wrap. 12. Repeat with remaining nori sheet and filling. 13. With a wet knife, cut each roll into bite-sized pieces. Serve with your favorite dipping sauce.

Per Serving: Calories 397; Total fat 11½g; Sodium 476mg; Total Carbs 66.4g; Fiber 3.2g; Sugars 10.6g; Protein 6.3g

Beef, Burdock & Perilla Sushi Rolls

Preparation Time: 20 minutes | Servings: 7

Ingredients:

3 tablespoons rice vinegar
2 tablespoons white sugar
1 teaspoon salt
7 cups cooked sushi rice
1 tablespoon sesame seeds, toasted
7 nori sheets

1 pound cooked beef, shredded
½ ounce Perilla leaves, stems removed
14 seasoned burdock root strips
7 yellow pickled radish strips
1 large cucumber, seeded and julienned
1 medium carrot, peeled and julienned

Preparation:

1. In a small-sized microwave-safe bowl, add vinegar, sugar and salt and microwave on high for around 30-45 seconds. 2. In a large-sized glass bowl, add rice and vinegar mixture and gently stir to combine. 3. Set aside to cool thoroughly. 4. After cooling, blend in sesame seeds. 5. Place 1 large-sized piece of plastic wrap onto a smooth surface. 6. Arrange 1 bamboo sushi mat over the plastic wrap. 7. Place 1 nori sheet on mat, shining-side-down, with the longer side of the nori facing you. 8. Place about 1 cup of rice over the nori, leaving a 1-inch border. 9. With your wet fingers, gently press the rice onto the nori in an even layer. 10. Arrange the beef, Perilla leaves, burdock root, radish, cucumber and carrot across the center of the rice. 11. Carefully lift up the bottom edge of the sushi mat and then fold it over the filling into a roll. 12. With the sushi mat, squeeze the roll tightly. 13. Carefully remove the mat and plastic wrap. 14. Repeat with remaining nori sheet and filling. 15. With a wet knife, cut each roll into bite-sized pieces. Serve with your favorite dipping sauce.

Per Serving: Calories 464; Total fat 4.4g; Sodium 606mg; Total Carbs 92.9g; Fiber 2.6g; Sugars 14.6g; Protein 15.3g

Pork Sushi Rolls

Preparation Time: 15 minutes | Cooking Time: 5 minutes | Servings: 3

Ingredients:

For the Rice:
¼ cup rice vinegar
3 tablespoons white sugar
For the Mayonnaise Sauce:
½ cup mayonnaise
2 tablespoons white sugar
For the Rolls:
3 nori sheets
1 cup pulled pork

2 teaspoons kosher salt
3 cups hot cooked sushi rice

2 teaspoons kosher salt

1 cup coleslaw
1 large avocado, peeled, pitted and sliced

Preparation:

1. For the rice: in a small-sized saucepan, add vinegar, sugar and salt over low heat and cook for around 3-5 minutes, stirring frequently. 2. In a large-sized bowl, add the cooked rice and vinegar mixture and toss to incorporate. Set aside to cool thoroughly. 3. For the mayonnaise sauce: in a small-sized bowl, add all ingredients and whisk to incorporate. 4. Place 1 large-sized piece of plastic wrap onto a smooth surface. 5. Arrange 1 bamboo sushi mat over the plastic wrap. 6. Place 1 nori sheet on mat, shining-side-down, with the longer side of the nori facing you. 7. Place about 1 cup of rice over the nori, leaving a 1-inch border. 8. With your wet fingers, gently press the rice onto the nori in an even layer. 9. Arrange the pulled pork, coleslaw and avocado across the center of the rice. 10. Carefully lift up the bottom edge of the sushi mat and then fold it over the filling into a roll. 11. With the sushi mat, squeeze the roll tightly. 12. Carefully remove the mat and plastic wrap. 13. Repeat with remaining nori sheets and filling. 14. With a wet knife, cut each roll into bite-sized pieces and drizzle with mayonnaise sauce. 15. Serve with your favorite dipping sauce.

Per Serving: Calories 454; Total fat 22.1g; Sodium 1276mg; Total Carbs 74.9g; Fiber 5.6g; Sugars 18.6g; Protein 10g

Trout & Watercress Sushi Rolls

Preparation Time: 15 minutes | Cooking Time: 5 minutes | Servings: 4

Ingredients:

2 tablespoons soy sauce
1 tablespoon rice vinegar
1 tablespoon honey
2 teaspoons wasabi paste
2 teaspoons fresh gingerroot, finely cut up
1 (14-ounce) skin on rainbow trout fillet
Non-stick baking spray

1 tablespoon sesame seeds, toasted
4 cups hot cooked sushi rice
¼ cup seasoned rice vinegar
4 nori sheets
½ of sweet yellow pepper, seeded and thinly sliced
1 carrot, peeled and thinly sliced
8 watercress stalks

Preparation:

1. In shallow dish, add soy sauce, 1 tablespoon of rice vinegar, honey, wasabi and ginger and blend to incorporate. 2. Add trout fillet and coat with mixture generously. 3. Refrigerate for around 2 hours. 4. For preheating: set your grill to medium-high heat. 5. Spray the grill grate with baking spray. 6. Place the trout onto the grill skin-side down. 7. Cover with the lid and cook for around 5 minutes, flipping once halfway through. 8. Remove from grill and transfer the trout fillet onto a plate. 9. Remove the skin of fillet and sprinkle with sesame seeds. 10. Chop the trout fillet into small pieces. 11. In a bowl, blend together the rice and vinegar. 12. Arrange 1 bamboo sushi mat over the plastic wrap. 13. Place 1 nori sheet on mat, shining-side-down, with the longer side of the nori facing you. 14. Place 1 cup of rice over the nori, leaving a 1-inch border. 15. With your wet fingers, gently press the rice onto the nori in an even layer. 16. Arrange the trout, yellow pepper, carrot and watercress across the center of the rice. 17. Carefully lift up the bottom edge of the sushi mat and then fold it over the filling into a roll. 18. With the sushi mat, squeeze the roll tightly. 19. Carefully remove the mat and plastic wrap. 20. Repeat with remaining nori sheet and filling. 21. With a wet knife, cut each roll into bite-size

Per Serving: Calories 349; Total fat 8.4g; Sodium 456mg; Total Carbs 47.9g; Fiber 1.2g; Sugars 3.6g; Protein 23.2g

---

BBQ Chicken Sushi Rolls

Preparation Time: 15 minutes | Servings: 2

Ingredients:

1 cup BBQ chicken, finely cut up
3 tablespoons mayonnaise
1 tablespoon fresh mixed herbs, cut up
Salt and ground black pepper, as desired
2 nori sheets

2 cups cooked and seasoned sushi rice (cooled)
½ of carrot, peeled and julienned
½ of cucumber, julienned
½ avocado, peeled, pitted and cut into strips
1 cup fresh baby spinach

Preparation:

1. In a bowl, add chicken, mayonnaise, herbs, salt and pepper and blend thoroughly. 2. Place 1 large-sized piece of plastic wrap onto a smooth surface. 3. Arrange 1 bamboo sushi mat over the plastic wrap. 4. Place 1 nori sheet on mat, shining-side-down, with the longer side of the nori facing you. 5. Place about 1 cup of rice over the nori, leaving a 1-inch border. 6. With your wet fingers, gently press the rice onto the nori in an even layer. 7. Place about 1 cup of rice over the nori, leaving a 1-inch border. 8. With your wet fingers, gently press the rice onto the nori in an even layer. 9. Spread the chicken mixture across center of rice. 10. Arrange the veggies across the center of the rice. 11. Carefully lift up the bottom edge of the sushi mat and then fold it over the filling into a roll. 12. With the sushi mat, squeeze the roll tightly. 13. Carefully remove the mat and plastic wrap. 14. Repeat with remaining nori sheets and filling. 15. With a wet knife, cut each roll into bite-sized pieces. Serve with your favorite dipping sauce.

Per Serving: Calories 523; Total Fat 4.4g; Sodium 525mg; Total Carbs 86.9g; Fiber 3.8g; Sugars 3.6g; Protein 32.1g

Chicken & Cucumber Sushi Rolls

Preparation Time: 15 minutes | Servings: 6

 Ingredients:

1 tablespoon sesame seeds, toasted
1 tablespoon granulated sugar
1 tablespoon soy sauce
½ teaspoon fresh ginger, grated

6 ounces cooked chicken, cut into pieces
4 nori sheets
4 cups cooked and seasoned sushi rice (cooled)
1 cucumber, cut into strips

Preparation:

1. Crush the sesame seeds and sugar with a mortar and pestle. 2. Transfer the crushed sesame seed mixture into a medium-sized bowl. 3. Add the soy sauce and ginger and blend to incorporate. 4. Add the chicken and toss to incorporate. 5. Place 1 large-sized piece of plastic wrap onto a smooth surface. 6. Arrange 1 bamboo sushi mat over the plastic wrap. 7. Place 1 nori sheet on mat, shining-side-down, with the longer side of the nori facing you. 8. Place about 1 cup of rice over the nori, leaving a 1-inch border. 9. With your wet fingers, gently press the rice onto the nori in an even layer. 10. Arrange the chicken mixture and cucumber across the center of the rice. 11. Carefully lift up the bottom edge of the sushi mat and then fold it over the filling into a roll. 12. With the sushi mat, squeeze the roll tightly. 13. Carefully remove the mat and plastic wrap. 14. Repeat with remaining nori sheets and filling. 15. With a wet knife, cut each roll into bite-sized pieces. Serve with your favorite dipping sauce.

Per Serving: Calories 203; Total Fat 4.4g; Sodium 425mg; Total Carbs 57.9g; Fiber 2.1g; Sugars 6.6g; Protein 16.1g

Chicken Tempura Sushi Rolls

Preparation Time: 20 minutes | Cooking Time: 5 minutes | Servings: 4

Ingredients:

¾ cup rice flour
2 teaspoons cornstarch
1 cup plus 2 tablespoons sparkling water
¼ teaspoons sea salt
4 nori sheets

4 cups cooked sushi rice (cooled)
1 large cooked chicken breast sliced or shredded
1 small cucumber thinly sliced lengthwise into sticks
1 small avocado pitted, peeled and sliced
Vegetable oil, for frying

Preparation:

1. In a medium bowl, add the flour, cornstarch, sparkling water and salt and whisk to incorporate. Set aside. 2. Place 1 large-sized piece of plastic wrap onto a smooth surface. 3. Arrange 1 bamboo sushi mat over the plastic wrap. 4. Place 1 nori sheet on mat, shining-side-down, with the longer side of the nori facing you. 5. Place 1 cup of rice over the nori, leaving a 1-inch border. 6. With your wet fingers, gently press the rice onto the nori in an even layer. 7. Arrange the cooked chicken, cucumber and avocado across the center of the rice. 8. Carefully lift up the bottom edge of the sushi mat and then fold it over the filling into a roll. 9. With the sushi mat, squeeze the roll tightly. 10. Carefully remove the mat and plastic wrap. 11. Repeat with remaining nori sheets and filling. 12. In a large-sized wok, heat oil over medium-high heat. 13. Dip the sushi rolls in the flour mixture. 14. Add the rolls into the wok and cook for around 4-6 minutes, flipping occasionally. 15. With a slotted spoon, transfer the tempura rolls onto a clean cutting board. 16. With a serrated knife, cut each roll into bite-sized pieces. Serve with your favorite dipping sauce.

Per Serving: Calories 373; Total Fat 12.4g; Sodium 505mg; Total Carbs 52.9g; Fiber 6.1g; Sugars 2.6g; Protein 20.1g

Beef & Asparagus Sushi Rolls

Preparation Time: 15 minutes | Servings: 4

Ingredients:

4 nori sheets
4 cups cooked and seasoned sushi rice (cooled)
4 ounces roast beef, thinly sliced

8 asparagus spears (seasoned and grilled)
4 ounces cream cheese, cut into slices
1 cup carrots, or julienned

Preparation:

1. Place 1 large-sized piece of plastic wrap onto a smooth surface. 2. Arrange 1 bamboo sushi mat over the plastic wrap. 3. Place 1 nori sheet on mat, shining-side-down, with the longer side of the nori facing you. 4. Place about 1 cup of rice over the nori, leaving a 1-inch border. 5. With your wet fingers, gently press the rice onto the nori in an even layer. 6. Arrange the roast beef, asparagus, cream cheese and carrots across the center of the rice. 7. Carefully lift up the bottom edge of the sushi mat and then fold it over the filling into a roll. 8. With the sushi mat, squeeze the roll tightly. 9. Carefully remove the mat and plastic wrap. 10. Repeat with remaining nori sheets and filling. 11. With a wet knife, cut each roll into bite-sized pieces. Serve with your favorite dipping sauce.

Per Serving: Calories 206; Total Fat 5.4g; Sodium 359mg; Total Carbs 35.9g; Fiber 1.1g; Sugars 1.6g; Protein 15.1g

Hot Dog & Kimchi Sushi Rolls

Preparation Time: 15 minutes | Servings: 4

Ingredients:

2 nori sheets
1 cup prepared sushi rice (follow this recipe or grab some from your local sushi spot!)

2 beef hot dogs, bun length
¼ cup kimchi, finely cut up with scissors
¼ cup avocado sliced thin

Preparation:

1. Cook hot dogs on the grill or in a pan on the stovetop until crispy on the outside. Split down the middle lengthwise, taking care to keep each hot dog in one piece. Set aside. 2. Lay a sheet of nori on a clean sushi rolling mat. Use wet hands to spread half the prepared rice across the nori, leaving about an inch of space at the edges. Next, nestle avocado across the rice. Top with hot dog, cut-side down. Lay kimchi across the seam of the hot dog. 3. Place 1 large-sized piece of plastic wrap onto a smooth surface. 4. Arrange 1 bamboo sushi mat over the plastic wrap. 5. Place 1 nori sheet on mat, shining-side-down, with the longer side of the nori facing you. 6. Place about 1 cup of rice over the nori, leaving a 1-inch border. 7. With your wet fingers, gently press the rice onto the nori in an even layer. 8. Arrange the slices of avocado across the center of the rice. 9. Carefully lift up the bottom edge of the sushi mat and then fold it over the filling into a roll. 10. With the sushi mat, squeeze the roll tightly. 11. Carefully remove the mat and plastic wrap. 12. Repeat with remaining nori sheets and filling. 13. With a wet knife, cut each roll into bite-sized pieces. Serve with your favorite dipping sauce.

Per Serving: Calories 343; Total Fat 8.4g; Sodium 125mg; Total Carbs 62.9g; Fiber 6.1g; Sugars 0.6g; Protein 6.1g

Chapter 3 Rice-Free Sushi Roll Recipes

Parmesan Cauliflower Rice Sushi Rolls

Preparation Time: 15 minutes | Cooking Time: 6 minutes | Servings: 2

Ingredients:

10 ounces cauliflower rice
Salt, as desired
½ teaspoon olive oil
3 cloves garlic, finely cut up
1-ounce Parmesan cheese, shredded
1 teaspoon lime juice

½ teaspoons soy sauce
½ teaspoons brown sugar
2 nori sheets
½ of cucumber, cut into thin strips
½ of carrot, peeled and cut into thin strips

Preparation:

1. In a large-sized bowl, add the cauliflower rice and sprinkle with salt. Set aside for around 15 minutes. 2. Rinse the cauliflower under running water to remove any excess salt. Again, drain the cauliflower rice. 3. Place the cauliflower trice over a damp muslin cloth and squeeze out the water. 4. In a wok, heat olive oil over medium heat and cook the garlic for around 2-40 seconds. 5. Add in the cauliflower rice and cook for around 2-3 minutes, stirring continuously. 6. Add in Parmesan cheese, lime juice, soy sauce and brown sugar and cook for around 1-2 minutes, stirring continuously. Remove from heat and set aside to cool. 7. Place 1 large-sized piece of plastic wrap onto a smooth surface. 8. Arrange 1 bamboo sushi mat over the plastic wrap. 9. Place 1 nori sheet on mat, shining-side-down, with the longer side of the nori facing you. 10. Place a layer of cauliflower rice over the nori, leaving a 1-inch border. 11. With your wet fingers, gently press the cauliflower rice onto the nori in an even layer. 12. Arrange the carrot and cucumber across the center of the cauliflower rice. 13. Carefully lift up the bottom edge of the sushi mat and then fold it over the filling into a roll. 14. With the sushi mat, squeeze the roll tightly. 15. Carefully remove the mat and plastic wrap. 16. Repeat with remaining nori sheets and filling. 17. With a wet knife, cut each roll into bite-sized pieces. Serve with your favorite dipping sauce.

Per Serving: Calories 120; Total fat 4.2g; Sodium 346mg; Total Carbs 13.9g; Fiber 4.6g; Sugars 5.6g; Protein 10.1g

Ground Beef Sushi Rolls

Preparation Time: 15 minutes | Cooking Time: 10 minutes | Servings: 4

Ingredients:

For the Beef:
1 lb. ground beef
1 large shallot, thin sliced lengthwise
3-4 cloves garlic, grated
3 tablespoons apple juice
2 tablespoons soy sauce
For the Rolls:
6 nori sheets
2 large carrots, peeled and julienned

3 teaspoons sesame oil, toasted
½ teaspoon onion powder
½ teaspoons coarse salt
1 tablespoon extra-virgin olive oil

1 English cucumber, julienned
1 butter lettuce head, torn

Preparation:

1. For the beef: in a large-sized bowl, add all ingredients except for olive oil and blend to incorporate. Refrigerate for around 20-30 minutes. 2. Heat olive oil into a wok over medium heat and cook the beef mixture for around 8-10 minutes. Remove from heat and set aside to cool. 3. Place 1 large-sized piece of plastic wrap onto a smooth surface. 4. Arrange 1 bamboo sushi mat over the plastic wrap. 5. Place 1 nori sheet on mat, shining-side-down, with the longer side of the nori facing you. 6. Place beef over the nori, leaving a 1-inch border. 7. With your wet fingers, gently press the quinoa onto the nori in an even layer. 8. Arrange the carrots, cucumber and lettuce across the center of the beef. 9. Carefully lift up the bottom edge of the sushi mat and then fold it over the filling into a roll. 10. With the sushi mat, squeeze the roll tightly. 11. Carefully remove the mat and plastic wrap. 12. Repeat with remaining nori sheets and filling. 13. With a wet knife, cut each roll into bite-sized pieces. Serve with your favorite dipping sauce.

Per Serving: Calories 179; Total fat 13.4g; Sodium 346mg; Total Carbs 5.9g; Fiber 0.6g; Sugars 2.6g; Protein 12.1g

Bulgur, Zucchini & Cilantro Sushi Rolls

Preparation Time: 15 minutes | Cooking Time: 5 minutes | Servings: 3

Ingredients:

2 tablespoons brown rice vinegar
1 tablespoon pure maple syrup
1½ teaspoons arrowroot powder
¼ teaspoon sea salt
1 cup bulgur

3 nori sheets
1 medium zucchini, seeded and cut into thin strips
1 small red onion, thinly sliced
1 cup carrots, peeled and shredded
12 fresh cilantro sprigs

Preparation:

1. In a small-sized bowl whisk together vinegar, maple syrup, arrowroot powder and salt. 2. In a small-sized saucepan, add 1½ cups of water and bring to a boil. 3. Stir in bulgur and vinegar mixture and immediately cover the pan. 4. Remove from heat and set aside, covered for around 20 minutes. 5. Drain tee bulgur and with a fork, fluff it. 6. Place 1 large-sized piece of plastic wrap onto a smooth surface. 7. Arrange 1 bamboo sushi mat over the plastic wrap. 8. Place 1 nori sheet on mat, shining-side-down, with the longer side of the nori facing you. 9. Place the bulgur over the nori, leaving a 1-inch border. 10. With your wet fingers, gently press the bulgur onto the nori in an even layer. 11. Arrange the zucchini, onion, carrots and cilantro across the center of the quinoa. 12. Carefully lift up the bottom edge of the sushi mat and then fold it over the filling into a roll. 13. With the sushi mat, squeeze the roll tightly. 14. Carefully remove the mat and plastic wrap. 15. Repeat with remaining nori sheets and filling. 16. With a wet knife, cut each roll into bite-sized pieces. Serve with your favorite dipping sauce.

Per Serving: Calories 174; Total fat 2.4g; Sodium 216mg; Total Carbs 28.9g; Fiber 2.6g; Sugars 10.6g; Protein 3.2g

Tuna, Cream Cheese & Avocado Sushi Rolls

Preparation Time: 15 minutes | Cooking Time: 10 minutes | Servings: 4

Ingredients:

1-pound cauliflower, cut into florets
5 ounces cream cheese, softened
1 tablespoon rice vinegar
3 teaspoons monkfruit sweetener
6 ounces ahi tuna, cubed

Dash of Sriracha
3 nori sheets
1 medium avocado, peeled, pitted and sliced thinly
2 tablespoons sesame seeds

Preparation:

1. In a clean food processor, add the cauliflower florets and pulse until rice like consistency is achieved. 2. In a pan of water, arrange a steamer insert and bring to a boil. 3. Place the cauliflower rice, into the steamer insert and steam, covered for around 10 minutes, stirring occasionally. 4. Transfer the steamed cauliflower rice into a bowl. 5. In the bowl of cauliflower rice, add cream cheese, rice vinegar and sweetener and blend to incorporate. 6. Cover the bowl and refrigerate for around 1 hour. 7. In another bowl, add the tuna and Sriracha and stir to blend. 8. Place 1 large-sized piece of plastic wrap onto a smooth surface. 9. Arrange 1 bamboo sushi mat over the plastic wrap. 10. Place 1 nori sheet on mat, shining-side-down, with the longer side of the nori facing you. 11. Place a layer of cauliflower rice over the nori, leaving a 1-inch border. 12. With your wet fingers, gently press the cauliflower rice onto the nori in an even layer. 13. Arrange the tuna mixture and avocado across the center of the cauliflower rice. 14. Carefully lift up the bottom edge of the sushi mat and then fold it over the filling into a roll. 15. With the sushi mat, squeeze the roll tightly. 16. Carefully remove the mat and plastic wrap. 17. Repeat with remaining nori sheets and filling. 18. With a wet knife, cut each roll into bite-sized pieces. Serve with your favorite dipping sauce.

Per Serving: Calories 500; Total fat 37.2g; Sodium 232mg; Total Carbs 20.8g; Fiber 9g; Sugars 4g; Protein 24.4g

Quinoa & Bean Sprout Sushi Rolls

Preparation Time: 15 minutes | Cooking Time: 25 minutes | Servings: 3

Ingredients:

1½ cups water
1 cup uncooked quinoa, rinsed
½ cup rice vinegar
2 teaspoons honey
2 teaspoons salt

3 nori sheets seaweed
1 avocado peeled, pitted and sliced
½ of large cucumber, peeled and cut into matchsticks
1 medium beet, peeled and grated
½ cup bean sprouts

Preparation:

1. In a medium-sized saucepan, place the water and quinoa over high heat and bring to a boil. 2. Reduce the heat to medium-low and cook, covered for around 15-20 minutes or until all the liquid is absorbed. 3. Remove the pan of quinoa from heat and stir in the vinegar, honey and salt. Set aside to cool thoroughly. 4. Place 1 large-sized piece of plastic wrap onto a smooth surface. 5. Arrange 1 bamboo sushi mat over the plastic wrap. 6. Place 1 nori sheet on mat, shining-side-down, with the longer side of the nori facing you. 7. Place ⅓ of the quinoa over the nori, leaving a 1-inch border. 8. With your wet fingers, gently press the quinoa onto the nori in an even layer. 9. Arrange the avocado, cucumber, beet and bean sprouts across the center of the quinoa. 10. Carefully lift up the bottom edge of the sushi mat and then fold it over the filling into a roll. 11. With the sushi mat, squeeze the roll tightly. 12. Carefully remove the mat and plastic wrap. 13. Repeat with remaining nori sheets and filling. 14. With a wet knife, cut each roll into bite-sized pieces. Serve with your favorite dipping sauce.

Per Serving: Calories 281; Total fat 12.5g; Sodium 1097mg; Total Carbs 46g; Fiber 8.6g; Sugars 8.6g; Protein 10.8g

Shrimp & Crab Sushi Rolls

Preparation Time: 20 minutes | Cooking Time: 5 minutes | Servings: 3

Ingredients:

1 medium cauliflower head
1 tablespoon avocado oil
2 teaspoons soy sauce
1 tablespoon rice vinegar
1 teaspoon salt

3 nori sheets
1 green mango, peeled, pitted and cut into thin strips
½ avocado, peeled, pitted and cut into thin strips
1 cup cooked crabmeat
3 medium cooked shrimp, cut up

Preparation:

1. In a clean food processor, add the cauliflower florets and pulse until rice like consistency is achieved. 2. Heat oil in a non-stick wok over medium-low heat and cook the cauliflower rice for around 2-3 minutes. 3. Add the soy sauce, vinegar and salt and cook for around 2 minutes. Remove from heat and set aside to cool. 4. Place 1 large-sized piece of plastic wrap onto a smooth surface. 5. Arrange 1 bamboo sushi mat over the plastic wrap. 6. Place 1 nori sheet on mat, shining-side-down, with the longer side of the nori facing you. 7. Place a layer of cauliflower rice over the nori, leaving a 1-inch border. 8. With your wet fingers, gently press the cauliflower rice onto the nori in an even layer. 9. Arrange the mango, avocado, crabmeat and shrimp across the center of the cauliflower rice. 10. Carefully lift up the bottom edge of the sushi mat and then fold it over the filling into a roll. 11. With the sushi mat, squeeze the roll tightly. 12. Carefully remove the mat and plastic wrap. 13. Repeat with remaining nori sheets and filling. 14. With a wet knife, cut each roll into bite-sized pieces. Serve with your favorite dipping sauce.

Per Serving: Calories 290; Total Fat 15.4g; Sodium 235mg; Total Carbs 10.9g; Fiber 5.1g; Sugars 2.6g; Protein 22.1g

Salmon & Cauliflower Sushi Rolls

Preparation Time: 20 minutes | Cooking Time: 6 minutes | Servings: 2

Ingredients:

10½ ounces cauliflower
1 tablespoon olive
2½ tablespoon cream cheese
½ tablespoon white wine vinegar
½ tablespoon white sesame seeds, toasted

2 nori sheets
7 ounces sushi grade raw salmon
½ of medium seedless cucumber, thinly sliced
½ of red bell pepper, seeded and thinly sliced
½ of large avocado, peeled, pitted and thinly sliced

Preparation:

1. In a clean food processor, add the cauliflower florets and pulse until rice like consistency is achieved. 2. Heat 1 tablespoon of oil in a non-stick wok over medium-low heat and cook the cauliflower rice for around 5-6 minutes. 3. Remove from heat and set aside to cool. 4. In a bowl, add the cauliflower rice, cream cheese, vinegar and sesame seeds and blend to incorporate. 5. Place 1 large-sized piece of plastic wrap onto a smooth surface. 6. Arrange 1 bamboo sushi mat over the plastic wrap. 7. Place 1 nori sheet on mat, shining-side-down, with the longer side of the nori facing you. 8. Place a layer of cauliflower rice over the nori, leaving a 1-inch border. 9. With your wet fingers, gently press the cauliflower rice onto the nori in an even layer. 10. Arrange the cucumber, pepper, avocado and salmon across the center of the cauliflower rice. 11. Carefully lift up the bottom edge of the sushi mat and then fold it over the filling into a roll. 12. With the sushi mat, squeeze the roll tightly. 13. Carefully remove the mat and plastic wrap. 14. Repeat with remaining nori sheets and filling. 15. With a wet knife, cut each roll into bite-sized pieces. Serve with your favorite dipping sauce.

Per Serving: Calories 304; Total fat 24.4g; Sodium 356mg; Total Carbs 14.9g; Fiber 10.6g; Sugars 3.8g; Protein 16.9g

Chicken & Greens Sushi Rolls

Preparation Time: 20 minutes | Cooking Time: 10 minutes | Servings: 2

Ingredients:

3 cups cauliflower rice
2 tablespoons rice vinegar
2 teaspoons tapioca flour
1 teaspoon olive oil
½ pound chicken cubed
3 tablespoons soy sauce
½ teaspoon sesame oil

½ teaspoon garlic powder
Pinch of salt and ground black pepper
2 nori sheets
1 cup fresh baby greens
½ avocado, peeled, pitted and thinly sliced
⅓ cucumber, thinly sliced

Preparation:

1. Heat the olive oil in a wok over medium heat and cook the cauliflower rice for around 3 minutes. 2. Add in the vinegar and a pinch of salt and cook for around 2 minutes. 3. Add in the tapioca four and blend thoroughly. 4. Remove from heat and set aside to cool. 5. In the same wok, add the chicken, soy sauce, sesame oil, garlic powder, pinch of salt and pepper over medium heat and cook for around 5 minutes, stirring occasionally. 6. Remove from heat and set aside to cool. 7. Squeeze out the water from cauliflower rice. 8. Place 1 large-sized piece of plastic wrap onto a smooth surface. 9. Arrange 1 bamboo sushi mat over the plastic wrap. 10. Place 1 nori sheet on mat, shining-side-down, with the longer side of the nori facing you. 11. Place a layer of cauliflower rice over the nori, leaving a 1-inch border. 12. With your wet fingers, gently press the cauliflower rice onto the nori in an even layer. 13. Arrange the chicken, greens, avocado and cucumber across the center of the cauliflower rice. 14. Carefully lift up the bottom edge of the sushi mat and then fold it over the filling into a roll. 15. With the sushi mat, squeeze the roll tightly. 16. Carefully remove the mat and plastic wrap. 17. Repeat with remaining nori sheet and filling. 18. With a wet knife, cut each roll into bite-sized pieces. Serve with your favorite dipping sauce.

Per Serving: Calories 353; Total Fat 28.4g; Sodium 425mg; Total Carbs 7.9g; Fiber 6.1g; Sugars 2.6g; Protein 21.1g

Quinoa & Lettuce Sushi Rolls

Preparation Time: 15 minutes | Cooking Time: 20 minutes | Servings: 5

Ingredients:

5 nori sheets
1 cup cooked quinoa
2 cups water
¼ teaspoon ground ginger
¼ teaspoons sea salt
1 tablespoon rice vinegar

1 tablespoon maple syrup
½ avocado, peeled, pitted and sliced
½ of cucumber, sliced
½ cup carrots, peeled and sliced
1 cup romaine lettuce, torn

Preparation:

1. In a medium-sized saucepan, place the water, quinoa, ground ginger and salt over high heat and bring to a boil. 2. Reduce the heat to medium-low and cook, covered for around 15 minutes or until all the liquid is absorbed. 3. Remove the pan of quinoa from heat and stir in the maple syrup and vinegar. Set aside to cool completely. 4. Place 1 large-sized piece of plastic wrap onto a smooth surface. 5. Arrange 1 bamboo sushi mat over the plastic wrap. 6. Place 1 nori sheet on mat, shining-side-down, with the longer side of the nori facing you. 7. Place a layer of quinoa over the nori, leaving a 1-inch border. 8. With your wet fingers, gently press the quinoa onto the nori in an even layer. 9. Arrange the lettuce, cucumber, avocado and carrot pieces across the center of the quinoa. 10. Carefully lift up the bottom edge of the sushi mat and then fold it over the filling into a roll. 11. With the sushi mat, squeeze the roll tightly. 12. Carefully remove the mat and plastic wrap. 13. Repeat with remaining nori sheets and filling. 14. With a wet knife, cut each roll into bite-sized pieces. Serve with your favorite dipping sauce.

Per Serving: Calories 190; Total Fat 6.4g; Sodium 125mg; Total Carbs 29.9g; Fiber 5.1g; Sugars 5.6g; Protein 6.1g

Quinoa & Tofu Sushi Rolls

Preparation Time: 20 minutes | Servings: 6

Ingredients:

3 tablespoons gochujang (Korean red chile paste)
2 tablespoons rice vinegar, divided
2 tablespoons soy sauce, divided
4 teaspoons brown rice syrup, divided
10 ounces extra-firm tofu, pressed, drained and cut into ¼-inch strips

3 cups cooked quinoa
6 nori sheets
2 tablespoons sesame seeds
1 avocado, peeled, pitted and sliced
1 cucumber, sliced

Preparation:

1. For the marinade: in a large-sized glass bowl, add the gochujang, half of soy sauce, vinegar and brown rice syrup and whisk to incorporate. 2. Add the tofu and coat with marinade. 3. Cover and refrigerate for 30 minutes. 4. In another large-sized bowl, add the quinoa, remaining vinegar, soy sauce and brown rice syrup and blend to incorporate. Set aside to cool thoroughly. 5. Place 1 large-sized piece of plastic wrap onto a smooth surface. 6. Arrange 1 bamboo sushi mat over the plastic wrap. 7. Place 1 nori sheet on mat, shining-side-down, with the longer side of the nori facing you. 8. Place a layer of quinoa over the nori, leaving a 1-inch border. 9. With your wet fingers, gently press the quinoa onto the nori in an even layer. 10. Sprinkle the top with sesame seeds. 11. Arrange the tofu, avocado and cucumber across the center of the quinoa. 12. Carefully lift up the bottom edge of the sushi mat and then fold it over the filling into a roll. 13. With the sushi mat, squeeze the roll tightly. 14. Carefully remove the mat and plastic wrap. 15. Repeat with remaining nori sheets and filling. 16. With a wet knife, cut each roll into bite-sized pieces. Serve with your favorite dipping sauce.

Per Serving: Calories 333; Total Fat 12.4g; Sodium 1005mg; Total Carbs 42.9g; Fiber 7.2g; Sugars 2.6g; Protein 15.9g

Bacon & Quinoa Sushi Rolls

Preparation Time: 15 minutes | Cooking Time: 20 minutes | Servings: 4

Ingredients:

1 cup quinoa, rinsed
3 nori sheets
1⅓ cups water
½ cup rice vinegar
2 tablespoons sugar

1 teaspoon salt
1 ripe avocado, peeled, pitted and sliced
½ cup sun-dried tomatoes in oil, drained
3 cooked bacon strips

Preparation:

1. In a medium-sized saucepan, place the water and quinoa over high heat and bring to a boil. 2. Reduce the heat to medium-low and cook, covered for around 12-15 minutes or until all the liquid is absorbed. 3. Meanwhile in a small-sized saucepan add the vinegar, sugar and salt over low heat and cook foe around 3-5 minutes. 4. Remove from heat and transfer into a glass bowl. 5. Remove the pan of quinoa from heat. 6. In the bowl of vinegar mixture, add the quinoa and blend to incorporate. Set aside to cool thoroughly. 7. Place 1 large-sized piece of plastic wrap onto a smooth surface. 8. Arrange 1 bamboo sushi mat over the plastic wrap. 9. Place 1 nori sheet on mat, shining-side-down, with the longer side of the nori facing you. 10. Place the quinoa over the nori, leaving a 1-inch border. 11. With your wet fingers, gently press the quinoa onto the nori in an even layer. 12. Arrange the avocado, tomatoes and bacon across the center of the quinoa. 13. Carefully lift up the bottom edge of the sushi mat and then fold it over the filling into a roll. 14. With the sushi mat, squeeze the roll tightly. 15. Carefully remove the mat and plastic wrap. 16. Repeat with remaining nori sheets and filling. 17. With a wet knife, cut each roll into bite-sized pieces. Serve with your favorite dipping sauce.

Per Serving: Calories 254; Total fat 14.4g; Sodium 556mg; Total Carbs 27.9g; Fiber 5.6g; Sugars 2.8g; Protein 8.1g

Salmon, Quinoa & Veggies Sushi Rolls

Preparation Time: 15 minutes | Servings: 4

Ingredients:

2 cups cooked quinoa
1½ tablespoons rice wine vinegar
1 tablespoon sesame seeds, toasted
4 nori sheets
½ medium ripe avocado, peeled, pitted and sliced

4oz smoked salmon, sliced
1 large carrot, peeled and shredded
1 red bell pepper, seeded and thinly sliced
1 large cucumber, seeded and cut in thin matchsticks

Preparation:

1. In a large-sized bowl, add the quinoa, vinegar and sesame seeds and blend to incorporate. Set aside to cool thoroughly. 2. Place 1 large-sized piece of plastic wrap onto a smooth surface. 3. Arrange 1 bamboo sushi mat over the plastic wrap. 4. Place 1 nori sheet on mat, shining-side-down, with the longer side of the nori facing you. 5. Place a layer of quinoa over the nori, leaving a 1-inch border. 6. With your wet fingers, gently press the quinoa onto the nori in an even layer. 7. Arrange the avocado, salmon, carrot, bell pepper and cucumber across the center of the quinoa. 8. Carefully lift up the bottom edge of the sushi mat and then fold it over the filling into a roll. 9. With the sushi mat, squeeze the roll tightly. 10. Carefully remove the mat and plastic wrap. 11. Repeat with remaining nori sheets and filling. 12. With a wet knife, cut each roll into bite-sized pieces. Serve with your favorite dipping sauce.

Per Serving: Calories 353; Total Fat 18.8g; Sodium 455mg; Total Carbs 46.9g; Fiber 9.1g; Sugars 8.6g; Protein 19.1g

Mixed Greens & Avocado Sushi Rolls

Preparation Time: 15 minutes | Servings: 4

Ingredients:

4 nori sheets
2 cups cauliflower rice
1 red bell pepper, seeded and thinly sliced
1 avocado, peeled, pitted and sliced

1 cup red cabbage, thinly sliced
2 scallions, thinly sliced
2 cups mixed greens, cut up

Preparation:

1. Place 1 large-sized piece of plastic wrap onto a smooth surface. 2. Arrange 1 bamboo sushi mat over the plastic wrap. 3. Place 1 nori sheet on mat, shining-side-down, with the longer side of the nori facing you. 4. Place a layer of cauliflower rice over the nori, leaving a 1-inch border. 5. With your wet fingers, gently press the cauliflower rice onto the nori in an even layer. 6. Arrange the bell pepper, avocado, cabbage, scallions and greens across the center of the cauliflower rice. 7. Carefully lift up the bottom edge of the sushi mat and then fold it over the filling into a roll. 8. With the sushi mat, squeeze the roll tightly. 9. Carefully remove the mat and plastic wrap. 10. Repeat with remaining nori sheets and filling. 11. With a wet knife, cut each roll into bite-sized pieces. Serve with your favorite dipping sauce.

Per Serving: Calories 114; Total fat 0.9g; Sodium 136mg; Total Carbs 7.9g; Fiber 2.6g; Sugars 1.3g; Protein 3.1g

Salmon & Alfalfa Sprout Sushi Rolls

Preparation Time: 15 minutes |Serving: 1

Ingredients:

2 ounces smoked salmon
½ teaspoon rice vinegar
1 nori sheet
1 tablespoon mayonnaise
¼ of cucumber, julienned

½ of carrot, peeled and julienned
¼ of red bell pepper, seeded and julienned
⅓ of avocado, peeled, pitted and sliced
¼ cup alfalfa sprouts

Preparation:

1. In a bowl, mix together the smoked salmon and vinegar. 2. Place 1 large-sized piece of plastic wrap onto a smooth surface. 3. Arrange 1 bamboo sushi mat over the plastic wrap. 4. Place the nori sheet on mat, shining-side-down, with the longer side of the nori facing you. 5. Spread mayonnaise over the nori, leaving a 1-inch border. 6. Arrange the salmon, cucumber, carrot, bell pepper, avocado and alfalfa sprouts across the center of the mayonnaise layer. 7. Carefully lift up the bottom edge of the sushi mat and then fold it over the filling into a roll. 8. With the sushi mat, squeeze the roll tightly. 9. Carefully remove the mat and plastic wrap. 10. With a wet knife, cut the roll into bite-sized pieces. Serve with your favorite dipping sauce.

Per Serving: Calories 234; Total fat 12.4g; Sodium 586mg; Total Carbs 15.1g; Fiber 6.6g; Sugars 5.6g; Protein 14.1g

Hearts of Palm Sushi Rolls

Preparation Time: 15 minutes | Servings: 4

Ingredients:

1 (14-ounce) can hearts of palm, drained and cut into thin strips
3 tablespoons mayonnaise
½ teaspoon paprika
¼ teaspoon salt

4 nori sheets
2-3 tablespoons sesame seeds, toasted
1 avocado, peeled, pitted and thinly sliced
½ of cucumber, cut into thin strips

Preparation:

1. In a large-sized bowl, add the hearts of palm, mayonnaise, paprika and salt and gently toss to incorporate. 2. Place 1 large-sized piece of plastic wrap onto a smooth surface. 3. Arrange 1 bamboo sushi mat over the plastic wrap. 4. Place 1 nori sheet on mat, shining-side-down, with the longer side of the nori facing you. 5. Place a layer of hearts of palm over the nori, leaving a 1-inch border. 6. With your wet fingers, gently press the heart of palm onto the nori in an even layer. 7. Sprinkle the top with sesame seeds. 8. Arrange the, avocado and cucumber across the center of the heart of palm layer. 9. Carefully lift up the bottom edge of the sushi mat and then fold it over the filling into a roll. 10. With the sushi mat, squeeze the roll tightly. 11. Carefully remove the mat and plastic wrap. 12. Repeat with remaining nori sheets and filling. 13. With a wet knife, cut each roll into bite-sized pieces. Serve with your favorite dipping sauce.

Per Serving: Calories 467; Total fat 18.4g; Sodium 236mg; Total Carbs 71.9g; Fiber 7.6g; Sugars 19.6g; Protein 9.1g

Quinoa & Cream Cheese Sushi Rolls

Preparation Time: 15 minutes | Cooking Time: 25 minutes | Servings: 5

Ingredients:

1 cup uncooked quinoa, rinsed
1½ cups water
½ cup seasoned rice vinegar
5 nori sheets
8 ounces cream cheese, cut into strips

⅓ cup sesame seeds, toasted
1 cucumber washed, peeled and cut into matchsticks
1 avocado washed, peeled and cut into long strips
2 carrots washed, peeled and cut into matchsticks or shredded

Preparation:

1. In a medium-sized saucepan, place the water and quinoa over high heat and bring to a boil. 2. Reduce the heat to medium-low and cook, covered for around 15-20 minutes or until all the liquid is absorbed. 3. Remove the pan of quinoa from heat and stir in thrice vinegar. 4. Immediately cover the pan of quinoa and set aside to cool completely. 5. Place 1 large-sized piece of plastic wrap onto a smooth surface. 6. Arrange 1 bamboo sushi mat over the plastic wrap. 7. Place 1 nori sheet on mat, shining-side-down, with the longer side of the nori facing you. 8. Place the quinoa over the nori, leaving a 1-inch border. 9. With your wet fingers, gently press the quinoa onto the nori in an even layer. 10. Place the cream cheese over the quinoa and sprinkle with sesame seeds. 11. Arrange the avocado, cucumber and carrot across the center of the quinoa. 12. Carefully lift up the bottom edge of the sushi mat and then fold it over the filling into a roll. 13. With the sushi mat, squeeze the roll tightly. 14. Carefully remove the mat and plastic wrap. 15. Repeat with remaining nori sheets and filling. 16. With a wet knife, cut each roll into bite-sized pieces. Serve with your favorite dipping sauce.

Per Serving: Calories 204; Total fat 7.4g; Sodium 306mg; Total Carbs 28.9g; Fiber 4.3g; Sugars 3.6g; Protein 6g

Soba Noodles Sushi Rolls

Preparation Time: 15 minutes | Servings: 10

Ingredients:

½ pound cooked soba noodles
¼ cup scallion
¼ cup pickled ginger, finely cut up
2 tablespoons light soy sauce
1 tablespoon rice wine vinegar

Wasabi oil, to taste
10 nori sheets
1 cucumber, peeled and finely julienned
2 bell peppers, seeded and julienned

Preparation:

1. In a bowl, add soba noodles, scallion, ginger, soy sauce, vinegar and wasabi and toss to incorporate. 2. Place 1 large-sized piece of plastic wrap onto a smooth surface. 3. Arrange 1 bamboo sushi mat over the plastic wrap. 4. Place 1 nori sheet on mat, shining-side-down, with the longer side of the nori facing you. 5. Place ½ of the noodles over the nori, leaving a 1-inch border. 6. With your wet fingers, gently press the noodles onto the nori in an even layer. 7. Arrange the cucumber and bell pepper across the center of the noodles. 8. Carefully lift up the bottom edge of the sushi mat and then fold it over the filling into a roll. 9. With the sushi mat, squeeze the roll tightly. 10. Carefully remove the mat and plastic wrap. 11. Repeat with remaining nori sheets and filling. 12. With a wet knife, cut each roll into bite-sized pieces. Serve with your favorite dipping sauce.

Per Serving: Calories 124; Total fat 1g; Sodium 476mg; Total Carbs 27.9g; Fiber 1.2g; Sugars 1.6g; Protein 6.1g

Crab & Quinoa Sushi Rolls

Preparation Time: 15 minutes | Servings: 4

Ingredients:

3 nori sheets
1 cup cooked quinoa
3 imitation crab sticks

½ of a large avocado, peeled, pitted and thinly sliced
½ of a cucumber, cut into thin slices

Preparation:

1. Place 1 large-sized piece of plastic wrap onto a smooth surface. 2. Arrange 1 bamboo sushi mat over the plastic wrap. 3. Place 1 nori sheet on mat, shining-side-down, with the longer side of the nori facing you. 4. Place ⅓ of the quinoa over the nori, leaving a 1-inch border. 5. With your wet fingers, gently press the quinoa onto the nori in an even layer. 6. Arrange the crab sticks, avocado and cucumber across the center of the quinoa. 7. Carefully lift up the bottom edge of the sushi mat and then fold it over the filling into a roll. 8. With the sushi mat, squeeze the roll tightly. Carefully remove the mat and plastic wrap. 9. Repeat with remaining nori sheets and filling. 10. With a wet knife, cut each roll into bite-sized pieces. Serve with your favorite dipping sauce.

Per Serving: Calories 286; Total fat 13.9g; Sodium 236mg; Total Carbs 26.9g; Fiber 5.6g; Sugars 3.1g; Protein 14.3

Sweet Potato, Peanuts & Jicama Sushi Rolls

Preparation Time: 15 minutes | Cooking Time: 7 minutes | Servings: 2

Ingredients:

2 nori sheets
2 small sweet potatoes
2-3 ounces enoki mushrooms

2 scallions, cut into matchsticks
¼ of small jicama, cut into matchsticks
¼ cup peanuts, roasted

Preparation:

1. With a fork, poke holes in each sweet potato. 2. In a microwave-safe dish, place the sweet potatoes and microwave on high for around 6 minutes. 3. Remove from microwave and set aside to cool slightly. 4. Remove the peel of sweet potatoes. 5. In a bowl, add the sweet potatoes and with a potato masher, mash them lightly. Set aside. 6. Remove the bottom of mushrooms and then separate into 5-10 small clusters. 7. Heat a small-sized, non-stick wok over high heat. 8. Cook the mushrooms with salt for around 1 minute, stirring twice. Remove from heat and set aside. 9. Place 1 large-sized piece of plastic wrap onto a smooth surface. 10. Arrange 1 bamboo sushi mat over the plastic wrap. 11. Place 1 nori sheet on mat, shining-side-down, with the longer side of the nori facing you. 12. Place a layer of mashed sweet potato over the nori, leaving a 1-inch border. 13. With your wet fingers, gently press the mashed sweet potato onto the nori in an even layer. 14. Arrange the jicama, mushrooms, scallions and peanuts across the center of the mashed sweet potato. 15. Carefully lift up the bottom edge of the sushi mat and then fold it over the filling into a roll. 16. With the sushi mat, squeeze the roll tightly. 17. Carefully remove the mat and plastic wrap. 18. Repeat with remaining nori sheets and filling. 19. With a wet knife, cut each roll into bite-sized pieces. Serve with your favorite dipping sauce.

Per Serving: Calories 233; Total Fat 1.8g; Sodium 125mg; Total Carbs 32.9g; Fiber 2.1g; Sugars 1.6g; Protein 5.1g

Yogurt & Veggie Sushi Rolls

Preparation Time: 15 minutes | Servings: 3

Ingredients:

3 nori sheets
½ cup plain Greek yogurt
1 avocado, peeled, pitted and sliced
1 teaspoon garlic, finely cut up

Salt and ground black pepper, as desired
1 carrot, peeled and sliced
1 cucumber, sliced
¼ cup red cabbage, shredded

Preparation:

1. In a bowl, add yogurt, half of avocado, garlic, salt and pepper and with a fork, mash to form a smooth mixture. 2. Place 1 large-sized piece of plastic wrap onto a smooth surface. 3. Arrange 1 bamboo sushi mat over the plastic wrap. 4. Place 1 nori sheet on mat, shining-side-down, with the longer side of the nori facing you. 5. Place a layer of yogurt mixture over the nori, leaving a 1-inch border. 6. With your wet fingers, gently press the yogurt mixture onto the nori in an even layer. 7. Arrange the remaining avocado, carrots, cucumber and cabbage across the center of yogurt mixture. 8. Carefully lift up the bottom edge of the sushi mat and then fold it over the filling into a roll. 9. With the sushi mat, squeeze the roll tightly. 10. Carefully remove the mat and plastic wrap. 11. Repeat with remaining nori sheets and filling. 12. With a wet knife, cut each roll into bite-sized pieces. Serve with your favorite dipping sauce.

Per Serving: Calories 143; Total Fat 11.4g; Sodium 125mg; Total Carbs 9.9g; Fiber 2.1g; Sugars 1.6g; Protein 6.1g

Miso Veggie Sushi Rolls

Preparation Time: 15 minutes | Servings: 3

Ingredients:

3 nori sheets
3 teaspoons miso paste, divided
1½ teaspoons hemp hearts, divided
½ avocado, peeled, pitted and sliced
2 radishes, julienned

1 small cucumber, julienned
2 carrots, peeled and julienned
1 small red bell pepper, seeded and julienned
1 batch enoki mushrooms

Preparation:

1. Place 1 large-sized piece of plastic wrap onto a smooth surface. 2. Arrange 1 bamboo sushi mat over the plastic wrap. 3. Place 1 nori sheet on mat, shining-side-down, with the longer side of the nori facing you. 4. Spread a thin layer of miso paste over the nori, leaving a 1-inch border. Top with hemp hearts. 5. With your wet fingers, gently press the hemp hearts and miso paste onto the nori in an even layer. 6. Arrange the avocado, cucumber, carrots, red pepper, radish and mushrooms across the center of the hemp hearts and miso paste. 7. Carefully lift up the bottom edge of the sushi mat and then fold it over the filling into a roll. 8. With the sushi mat, squeeze the roll tightly. 9. Carefully remove the mat and plastic wrap. 10. Repeat with remaining nori sheets and filling. 11. With a wet knife, cut each roll into bite-sized pieces. Serve with your favorite dipping sauce.

Per Serving: Calories 127; Total Fat 8.4g; Sodium 675mg; Total Carbs 11.9g; Fiber 5.1g; Sugars 4.6g; Protein 4.6g

Tofu, Carrot & Cucumber Sushi Rolls

Preparation Time: 15 minutes | Cooking Time: 10 minutes | Servings: 6

Ingredients:

10 ounces super firm tofu, pressed, drained and sliced
1 scallion, roughly cut up
4 tablespoons rice vinegar
2 teaspoons sesame oil
1 teaspoon salt

¼ teaspoon garlic powder
6 nori sheets
1 large carrot, peeled and sliced
2 cucumbers, sliced

Preparation:

1. In a food processor, add the tofu, scallion, vinegar, sesame oil, salt and garlic powder and process to form a slight crumbly mixture. 2. Place 1 large-sized piece of plastic wrap onto a smooth surface. 3. Arrange 1 bamboo sushi mat over the plastic wrap. 4. Place 1 nori sheet on mat, shining-side-down, with the longer side of the nori facing you. 5. Place a layer of tofu mixture over the nori, leaving a 1-inch border. 6. With your wet fingers, gently press the tofu mixture onto the nori in an even layer. 7. Arrange the slices of carrot and cucumber across the center of the tofu mixture. 8. Carefully lift up the bottom edge of the sushi mat and then fold it over the filling into a roll. 9. With the sushi mat, squeeze the roll tightly. 10. Carefully remove the mat and plastic wrap. 11. Repeat with remaining nori sheets and filling. 12. With a wet knife, cut each roll into bite-sized pieces. Serve with your favorite dipping sauce.

Per Serving: Calories 125; Total Fat 3.2g; Sodium 346mg; Total Carbs 12.9g; Fiber 3.6g; Sugars 4.6g; Protein 11.1g

Salmon & Avocado Sushi Rolls

Preparation Time: 15 minutes | Cooking Time: 3 minutes | Servings: 4

Ingredients:

3 cups cauliflower rice
1 teaspoon xanthan gum
4 nori sheets

½ pound sushi grade salmon
1 large avocado, peeled, pitted and sliced
½ cucumber, sliced

Preparation:

1. Heat a non-stick wok over medium heat and stir-fry the cauliflower rice with xanthan gum for around 2-3 minutes. 2. Remove from heat and set aside to cool thoroughly. 3. Place 1 large-sized piece of plastic wrap onto a smooth surface. 4. Arrange 1 bamboo sushi mat over the plastic wrap. 5. Place 1 nori sheet on mat, shining-side-down, with the longer side of the nori facing you. 6. Place a layer of cauliflower rice over the nori, leaving a 1-inch border. 7. With your wet fingers, gently press the cauliflower rice onto the nori in an even layer. 8. Arrange the salmon, avocado and cucumber across the center of the cauliflower rice. 9. Carefully lift up the bottom edge of the sushi mat and then fold it over the filling into a roll. 10. With the sushi mat, squeeze the roll tightly. 11. Carefully remove the mat and plastic wrap. 12. Repeat with remaining nori sheets and filling. 13. With a wet knife, cut each roll into bite-sized pieces. Serve with your favorite dipping sauce.

Per Serving: Calories 324; Total fat 20.4g; Sodium 236mg; Total Carbs 21.9g; Fiber 6.2g; Sugars 4.6g; Protein 20.8g

Veggies & Avocado Sushi Rolls

Preparation Time: 15 minutes | Cooking Time: 6 minutes | Servings: 2

Ingredients:

3½ cups cauliflower rice
2 tablespoons rice vinegar
1 teaspoon light honey
½ teaspoon sea salt
2 teaspoons tapioca starch

2 nori sheets
1 small carrot, peeled and julienned
¼ English cucumber, julienned
½ avocado, peeled, pitted and cut into 6 slices

Preparation:

1. Heat a non-stick wok over medium high heat and stir-fry the cauliflower for around 3 minutes. 2. Blend in vinegar, honey and salt and stir-fry for around 2 minutes. 3. Add the tapioca starch and stir-fry for around 1 minute. 4. Remove from heat and place the cooked cauliflower rice onto a kitchen towel to cool. 5. Place 1 large-sized piece of plastic wrap onto a smooth surface. 6. Arrange 1 bamboo sushi mat over the plastic wrap. 7. Place 1 nori sheet on mat, shining-side-down, with the longer side of the nori facing you. 8. Place a layer of cauliflower rice over the nori, leaving a 1-inch border. 9. With your wet fingers, gently press the cauliflower rice onto the nori in an even layer. 10. Arrange the carrot, cucumber and avocado across the center of the cauliflower rice. 11. Carefully lift up the bottom edge of the sushi mat and then fold it over the filling into a roll. 12. With the sushi mat, squeeze the roll tightly. 13. Carefully remove the mat and plastic wrap. 14. Repeat with remaining nori sheets and filling. 15. With a wet knife, cut each roll into bite-sized pieces. Serve with your favorite dipping sauce.

Per Serving: Calories 170; Total fat 6.4g; Sodium 672mg; Total Carbs 18.9g; Fiber 8.6g; Sugars 9.6g; Protein 6g

Quinoa & Mango Sushi Rolls

Preparation Time: 15 minutes | Servings: 5

Ingredients:

2½ cups hot cooked quinoa
3 tablespoons rice vinegar
1 teaspoon cane sugar
½ teaspoons sea salt
5 nori sheets

1 avocado, peeled, pitted and sliced
½ cucumber, julienned
1 ripe mango, peeled, pitted and sliced
2 scallions, finely cut up

Preparation:

1. In a large-sized bowl, add the vinegar, sugar and salt and whisk to incorporate. 2. Add the quinoa and blend thoroughly. Set aside to cool thoroughly. 3. Place 1 large-sized piece of plastic wrap onto a smooth surface. 4. Arrange 1 bamboo sushi mat over the plastic wrap. 5. Place 1 nori sheet on mat, shining-side-down, with the longer side of the nori facing you. 6. Place a layer of quinoa over the nori, leaving a 1-inch border. 7. With your wet fingers, gently press the quinoa onto the nori in an even layer. 8. Arrange the avocado, cucumber, mango and scallions across the center of the quinoa. 9. Carefully lift up the bottom edge of the sushi mat and then fold it over the filling into a roll. 10. With the sushi mat, squeeze the roll tightly. 11. Carefully remove the mat and plastic wrap. 12. Repeat with remaining nori sheets and filling. 13. With a wet knife, cut each roll into bite-sized pieces. Serve with your favorite dipping sauce.

Per Serving: Calories 283; Total Fat 13.4g; Sodium 125mg; Total Carbs 37.9g; Fiber 6.9g; Sugars 3.6g; Protein 8.3g

Cream Cheese Veggies Sushi Rolls

Preparation Time: 15 minutes | Cooking Time: 7 minutes | Servings: 2

Ingredients:

1 cup cauliflower florets
1 tablespoon coconut oil
2 nori sheets

½ medium avocado, peeled, pitted and cut into thin slices
1½ ounces cream cheese, cut into thin slices
¼ cup cucumber, cut into thin slices

Preparation:

1. In a clean food processor, add the cauliflower florets and pulse until rice like consistency is achieved. 2. In a wok, melt coconut oil over medium-high heat and cook the cauliflower rice for around 5-7 minutes, stirring frequently. 3. Transfer the cauliflower rice into bowl and set aside. 4. Place 1 large-sized piece of plastic wrap onto a smooth surface. 5. Arrange 1 bamboo sushi mat over the plastic wrap. 6. Place 1 nori sheet on mat, shining-side-down, with the longer side of the nori facing you. 7. Place a layer of cauliflower rice over the nori, leaving a 1-inch border. 8. With your wet fingers, gently press the cauliflower rice onto the nori in an even layer. 9. Arrange the slices of avocado, cream cheese and cucumber across the center of the cauliflower rice10. Carefully lift up the bottom edge of the sushi mat and then fold it over the filling into a roll. 11. With the sushi mat, squeeze the roll tightly. 12. Carefully remove the mat and plastic wrap. 13. Repeat with remaining nori sheets and filling. 14. With a wet knife, cut each roll into bite-sized pieces. Serve with your favorite dipping sauce.

Per Serving: Calories 233; Total Fat 23.4g; Sodium 155mg; Total Carbs 9.9g; Fiber 5.1g; Sugars 1.6g; Protein 5.1g

Smoked Salmon & Cream Cheese Sushi Rolls

Preparation Time: 15 minutes | Cooking Time: 6 minutes | Servings: 5

Ingredients:

16 ounces cauliflower
1 teaspoon olive oil
1 tablespoon soy sauce
6 ounces cream cheese, softened
1-2 tablespoons rice vinegar

5 nori sheets
1 cucumber, cut into thin strips
½ medium avocado, peeled, pitted and sliced
5 ounces smoked salmon

Preparation:

1. In a clean food processor, add the cauliflower florets and pulse until rice like consistency is achieved. 2. Heat oil in a non-stick wok over medium-low heat and cook the cauliflower rice with soy sauce for around 5-6 minutes. Remove from heat and set aside to cool. 3. In a bowl, add the cauliflower rice, cream cheese and vinegar and blend to incorporate. 4. Place 1 large-sized piece of plastic wrap onto a smooth surface. 5. Arrange 1 bamboo sushi mat over the plastic wrap. 6. Place 1 nori sheet on mat, shining-side-down, with the longer side of the nori facing you. 7. Place a layer of cauliflower rice over the nori, leaving a 1-inch border. 8. With your wet fingers, gently press the cauliflower rice onto the nori in an even layer. 9. Arrange the cucumber, avocado and salmon across the center of the cauliflower rice. 10. Carefully lift up the bottom edge of the sushi mat and then fold it over the filling into a roll. 11. With the sushi mat, squeeze the roll tightly. 12. Carefully remove the mat and plastic wrap. 13. Repeat with remaining nori sheets and filling. 14. With a wet knife, cut each roll into bite-sized pieces. Serve with your favorite dipping sauce.

Per Serving: Calories 350; Total Fat 24.4g; Sodium 225mg; Total Carbs 12.9g; Fiber 6.1g; Sugars 3.6g; Protein 19.1g

Tuna, Chives & Cucumber Sushi Rolls

Preparation Time: 15 minutes | Servings: 4

Ingredients:

1-pound fresh yellowfin tuna steak, cut into ¼-inch pieces
3 tablespoons fresh chives, finely cut up
¼ cup low-sodium soy sauce
2 tablespoons rice wine vinegar
2 tablespoons sesame oil

½ teaspoons salt
¼ teaspoon ground black pepper
4 nori sheets
3 cucumbers, sliced thinly
1 teaspoon sesame seeds, toasted

Preparation:

1. In a medium-sized bowl, add the tuna, chives, soy sauce, vinegar, sesame oil, salt and pepper and blend to incorporate. Cover the bowl and refrigerate for 30-50 minutes. 2. Slice the cucumbers lengthwise, as thinly as possible into approximately 5-inch lengths. Season with salt and pepper, as desired. 3. Place 1 heaping teaspoon of the tuna tartar on one end of the cucumber slice. Roll up. The cucumber, when very thinly sliced, will stick together and stay rolled without a toothpick. Continue making rolls with the remaining ingredients. 4. Top each roll with ¼ teaspoon dollop of spicy mayonnaise and a sprinkling of sesame seeds. 5. Spoon some shiso mayo over the top of the sushi rolls and garnish each with ¼ to ½ teaspoon sesame seeds if desired. Serve with soy sauce, ginger and wasabi if desired. Serve with your favorite dipping sauce.

Per Serving: Calories 343; Total Fat 8.4g; Sodium 125mg; Total Carbs 62.9g; Fiber 6.1g; Sugars 0.6g; Protein 6.1g

Herbed Crab Sushi Rolls

Preparation Time: 15 minutes | Servings: 4

Ingredients:

½ pound fresh crabmeat, picked over
1 shallot, finely cut up
¼ cup fresh cilantro, cut up
¼ cup fresh leaf parsley, cut up
¼ cup fresh basil, cut up
½ tablespoon honey

½ tablespoon Dijon mustard
1 tablespoon lemon juice
½ tablespoon canola oil
Salt and ground white pepper, as desired
4 nori sheets

Preparation:

1. In a bowl, add all ingredients except for nori and blend to incorporate thoroughly. 2. Place 1 large-sized piece of plastic wrap onto a smooth surface. 3. Arrange 1 bamboo sushi mat over the plastic wrap. 4. Place 1 nori sheet on mat, shining-side-down, with the longer side of the nori facing you. 5. Place a layer of crab mixture over the nori, leaving a 1-inch border. 6. With your wet fingers, gently press the crab mixture onto the nori in an even layer. 7. Carefully lift up the bottom edge of the sushi mat and then fold it over the filling into a roll. 8. With the sushi mat, squeeze the roll tightly. 9. Carefully remove the mat and plastic wrap. 10. Repeat with remaining nori sheets and filling. 11. With a wet knife, cut each roll into bite-sized pieces. Serve with your favorite dipping sauce.

Per Serving: Calories 294; Total Fat 21.4g; Sodium 346mg; Total Carbs 12.9g; Fiber 8.6g; Sugars 3.1g; Protein 15.9g

Shrimp & Cauliflower Sushi Rolls

Preparation Time: 15 minutes | Cooking Time: 10 minutes | Servings: 4

Ingredients:

1 tablespoon olive oil
2 cups cauliflower rice
3 ounces cream cheese softened
½ tablespoon rice vinegar

5 nori sheets
½ cucumber, seeded and cut into thin strips
1 avocado, peeled, pitted and thinly sliced
½ pound cooked shrimp, cut into pieces

Preparation:

1. Heat oil in a non-stick wok over medium-low heat and cook the cauliflower rice for around 5-6 minutes. Remove from heat and set aside to cool. 2. In a bowl, add the cauliflower rice, cream cheese and vinegar and blend to incorporate. 3. Place 1 large-sized piece of plastic wrap onto a smooth surface. 4. Arrange 1 bamboo sushi mat over the plastic wrap. 5. Place 1 nori sheet on mat, shining-side-down, with the longer side of the nori facing you. 6. Place a layer of cauliflower rice over the nori, leaving a 1-inch border. 7. With your wet fingers, gently press the cauliflower rice onto the nori in an even layer. 8. Arrange the avocado, cucumber and shrimp across the center of the cauliflower rice. 9. Carefully lift up the bottom edge of the sushi mat and then fold it over the filling into a roll. 10. With the sushi mat, squeeze the roll tightly. 11. Carefully remove the mat and plastic wrap. 12. Repeat with remaining nori sheets and filling. 13. With a wet knife, cut each roll into bite-sized pieces. Serve with your favorite dipping sauce.

Per Serving: Calories 196; Total Fat 14.4g; Sodium 509mg; Total Carbs 6.9g; Fiber 3.6g; Sugars 2.6g; Protein 13.1g

Chapter 4 Baked Sushi Recipes

Chicken Sushi Cups

Preparation Time: 15 minutes | Cooking Time: 16 minutes | Servings: 6

Ingredients:

3 boneless chicken breasts, cut into small cubes
1½ tablespoons mayonnaise
1 teaspoon avocado oil
¼ teaspoon paprika
Salt and ground black pepper, as desired

1½ cups hot cooked rice
2 teaspoons rice vinegar
2 nori sheets, cut into 6 (3½-inch) squares
1 tablespoon fresh chives, cut up

Preparation:

1. For preheating: set your oven at 400ºF. 2. In a bowl, add the rice and vinegar and blend thoroughly. Set aside to cool slightly. 3. In a bowl, add the chicken cubes, mayonnaise, oil, paprika, salt and pepper and blend to incorporate thoroughly. 4. Arrange the nori squares onto a smooth surface. 5. Place 1 tablespoon of warm rice on top of each nori square. 6. With your hands, press down the rice. 7. Carefully place each nori square with rice into muffin cups. 8. Place 1 tablespoon of chicken cubes on top of rice. Bake for around 15 minutes. 9. After 15 minutes of cooking, set your oven to broiler. 10. Broil for around 1-1½ minutes. 11. Remove the muffin tin from oven and set aside to cool slightly. 12. Carefully remove sushi cups from muffin cups and transfer onto a serving platter. 13. Garnish with chives and serve.

Per Serving: Calories 220; Total fat 7.4g; Sodium 166mg; Total Carbs 13.9g; Fiber 0.5g; Sugars 0.4g; Protein 26.1g

---

Buffalo Chicken Sushi Cups

Preparation Time: 15 minutes | Cooking Time: 15 minutes | Servings: 16

Ingredients:

4 nori sheets, cut into fourths
2½ cups cooked white rice
1½ cups cooked chicken, shredded
¾ cup buffalo sauce

1 avocado, peeled, pitted and cut into small pieces
2 small cucumbers, cut into small pieces
2 carrots, peeled and cut into small pieces
½ cup scallion, cut into small pieces

Preparation:

1. For preheating: set your oven at 350ºF. 2. Arrange the nori squares onto a smooth surface. 3. Place 1 tablespoon of warm rice on top of each nori square. 4. With your hands, press down the rice. 5. Carefully place each nori square with rice into muffin cups. 6. Top each with chicken, followed by buffalo sauce. 7. Bake for around 15 minutes. 8. Remove the muffin tin from oven and set aside to cool slightly. 9. Carefully remove sushi cups from muffin cups and transfer onto a serving platter. 10. Top with avocado, cucumbers, carrot and scallion and serve.

Per Serving: Calories 84; Total fat 3.6g; Sodium 376mg; Total Carbs 18.9g; Fiber 2.6g; Sugars 1.6g; Protein 5.2g

---

Flavorful Salmon Sushi Cups

Preparation Time: 15 minutes | Cooking Time: 15 minutes | Servings: 12

Ingredients:

Non-stick baking spray
1 (1½-pound) skinless salmon fillet, cut into ½-inch cubes
2 scallions, thinly sliced
4 tablespoons mayonnaise, divided
2¼ teaspoons Sriracha, divided

1 teaspoon sesame oil, toasted
Salt, as desired
3 nori sheets, quartered
2 cups cooked sushi rice
2 teaspoons sesame seeds

Preparation:

1. For preheating: arrange a rack in upper third of oven. Set your oven at 400ºF. 2. Lightly spray a 12-cup muffin tin with baking spray. 3. In a large-sized bowl, add the salmon, scallions, 2 tablespoons of mayonnaise, 2 teaspoons of Sriracha, sesame oil and salt and toss to incorporate. 4. Arrange the nori squares onto a smooth surface. 5. Place 1 tablespoon of warm rice on top of each nori square. 6. With your hands, press down the rice. 7. Top each with salmon mixture. 8. Bake for around 11 minutes. 9. After 11 minutes of cooking, set your oven to broiler. 10. Broil for around 2-4 minutes. 11. Remove the muffin tin from oven and set aside to cool slightly. 12. Meanwhile, in a small-sized bowl, add remaining mayonnaise and Sriracha and blend thoroughly. 13. Carefully remove sushi cups from muffin cups and transfer onto a serving platter. 14. Drizzle with mayonnaise mixture. 15. Sprinkle with sesame seeds and serve.

Per Serving: Calories 205; Total fat 14.4g; Sodium 226mg; Total Carbs 9.9g; Fiber 1.2g; Sugars 1.6g; Protein 13.2g

Tofu & Mushroom Sushi Bake

Preparation Time: 15 minutes | Cooking Time: 30 minutes | Servings: 6

Ingredients:

3 cups king oyster mushrooms, finely cut up
2 tablespoon soy sauce
10½ ounces silken tofu, pressed, drained and cut up
2 tablespoon mayonnaise
2 tablespoon Sriracha

2 tablespoons rice vinegar, divided
3 cups cooked sushi rice
2 teaspoon sesame oil, toasted
½ teaspoon salt
2 nori sheets, crushed

Preparation:

1. For preheating: set your oven at 375ºF. 2. Grease a 9x9-inch baking dish with baking spray. 3. In a non-stick saucepan, add mushrooms and soy sauce over medium heat and cook for around 10-15 minutes. 4. Meanwhile, the in a large bowl, add the tofu, Sriracha, 1 tablespoon of vinegar and mayonnaise and with a fork, mash to form a smooth mixture. 5. Add the cooked mushrooms into the bowl with tofu mix and blend to incorporate thoroughly. 6. In another bowl, add the rice, remaining vinegar, sesame oil and salt and blend thoroughly. 7. Place the rice in the bottom of baking dish and sprinkle with nori sheet. 8. Top with tofu mixture evenly. 9. Bake for around 10-15 minutes. 10. Serve warm.

Per Serving: Calories 138; Total fat 11.4g; Sodium 256mg; Total Carbs 18.9g; Fiber 2.1g; Sugars 1.3g; Protein 5.1g

Shrimp Sushi Bake

Preparation Time: 15 minutes | Cooking Time: 15 minutes | Servings: 2

Ingredients:

2 tablespoons cream cheese, softened
2 tablespoons mayonnaise
1 tablespoon soy sauce
Sriracha, as desired

½ teaspoon sesame oil
½ pound jumbo shrimp, peeled, deveined and cut into small pieces
1 cup cooked sushi rice
1 nori sheet, cut into squares

Preparation:

1. For preheating: set your oven at 400ºF. 2. In a large-sized bowl, add the cream cheese, mayonnaise, soy sauce, Sriracha and sesame oil and blend to incorporate thoroughly. 3. Add the shrimp and coat with mixture generously. 4. In the bottom of a small-sized baking dish, place the rice and with the back of a spoon, press downwards. 5. Place the shrimp mixture on top of rice evenly. 6. Bake for around 12 minutes. 7. After 12 minutes of cooking, set your oven to broiler. 8. Broil for around 2-3 minutes. 9. Enjoy the shrimp mixture over nori.

Per Serving: Calories 534; Total fat 22.4g; Sodium 896mg; Total Carbs 46.9g; Fiber 4.6g; Sugars 1.6g; Protein 22.2g

Crab Sushi Bake

Preparation Time: 15 minutes | Cooking Time: 15 minutes | Servings: 6

Ingredients:

3 cups rice cooked sushi rice
¼ cup rice vinegar
½ tablespoons white sugar
1 teaspoon salt
8 ounces imitation crab, shredded and cut up

½ cup cream cheese, softened
½ cup mayonnaise
¼ cup nori sheet, crushed
3 packages roasted seaweed snacks

Preparation:

1. For preheating: set your oven at 425ºF. 2. In a small-sized saucepan, add the vinegar, sugar and salt over medium-low heat and cook for around 2-3 minutes, stirring continuously. 3. In a large-sized bowl, add the cooked rice and vinegar mixture and blend to incorporate. Set aside to cool thoroughly. 4. In a bowl, add crab, cream cheese and mayonnaise and blend to incorporate thoroughly. 5. Place the rice in the bottom of baking dish and sprinkle with crushed nori. 6. Place the crab mixture on top. 7. Bake for around 10-15 minutes. 8. Serve warm with the topping of seaweed snack.

Per Serving: Calories 477; Total fat 30.4g; Sodium 986mg; Total Carbs 40.9g; Fiber 4.6g; Sugars 4.6g; Protein 10.4g

Salmon & Yogurt Sushi Bake

Preparation Time: 15 minutes | Cooking Time: 10 minutes | Servings: 6

Ingredients:

2 teaspoon sesame oil
3 cups cooked sushi rice
2-3 tablespoons seasoned rice vinegar
12 ounces canned salmon
1 cup carrots, peeled and grated

½ cup plain Greek yogurt
¼ cup mayonnaise
1 tablespoon lime juice
Furikake seasoning, as desired

Preparation:

1. For preheating: set your oven at 400ºF. 2. Spray a baking dish with a little sesame oil. 3. In a bowl, add cooked rice, vinegar and remaining sesame oil and blend thoroughly. 4. In another large-sized bowl, add salmon, carrots, yogurt, mayonnaise and lime juice and blend to incorporate thoroughly. 5. Place the rice into the prepared baking dish and spread in an even layer. 6. Sprinkle the rice with furikake seasoning. 7. Spread the salmon mixture on top of rice. 8. Bake for around 10 minutes. 9. Serve warm.

Per Serving: Calories 264; Total fat 12.4g; Sodium 336mg; Total Carbs 22.9g; Fiber 1.6g; Sugars 3.2g; Protein 18.2g

Crab & Mango Sushi Cups

Preparation Time: 15 minutes | Cooking Time: 20 minutes | Servings: 12

Ingredients:

3 cups cooked sushi rice
2 tablespoons rice vinegar
½ tablespoon sesame oil
2 teaspoons white sugar
½ teaspoon salt
5 imitation crab sticks, cut up

1 cup ripe mango, peeled, pitted and cut up
¾ cup cucumber, cut up
3½ ounces cream cheese, softened
⅓ cup mayonnaise
3 large nori sheets, quartered

Preparation:

1. For preheating: set your oven at 400ºF. 2. Spray a muffin tin with baking spray. 3. In a bowl, add the cooked rice, vinegar, sesame oil, sugar and salt and blend to incorporate. 4. In another bowl, add the crab, mango, cucumber, cream cheese and mayonnaise and blend to incorporate. 5. Arrange a nori square into each prepared muffin cup. 6. Place about 3-4 tablespoons of cooked rice on top of nori piece and press slightly. 7. Top each cup with mango mixture. 8. Bake for around 15-20 minutes. 9. Remove the muffin tin from oven and set aside to cool slightly. 10. Carefully remove sushi cups from muffin cups and transfer onto a serving platter. 11. Serve warm.

Per Serving: Calories 234; Total fat 10.4g; Sodium 506mg; Total Carbs 23.9g; Fiber 2.6g; Sugars 8.6g; Protein 10.4g

Crab Sushi Cups

Preparation Time: 15 minutes | Cooking Time: 15 minutes | Servings: 12

Ingredients:

Non-stick baking spray
¼ cup rice vinegar
½ tablespoon white sugar
1 teaspoon salt
8 ounces imitation crab, shredded
½ cup mayonnaise

½ cup cream cheese, softened
1 cup cooked short-grain rice
¼ cup furikake
1 cucumber, sliced
1 avocado, peeled, pitted and cubed

Preparation:

1. For preheating: set your oven at 425ºF. 2. Spray the muffin tin with baking spray. 3. In a small-sized saucepan, add vinegar, sugar and salt over low heat and cook for around 3-5 minutes, stirring frequently. 4. In a bowl, add crab, mayonnaise and cream cheese and blend to form a smooth mixture. 5. In a large-sized bowl, add the cooked rice and vinegar mixture and toss to incorporate. Set aside to cool slightly. 6. Place the rice into prepared muffin cups and spread evenly. 7. Sprinkle the rice with half of the furikake. 8. Top with crab mixture and sprinkle with remaining furikake. 9. Bake for around 10-15 minutes. 10. Remove the muffin tin from oven and set aside to cool slightly. 11. Carefully remove sushi cups from muffin cups and transfer onto a serving platter. 12. Top with cucumber and avocado and serve.

Per Serving: Calories 222; Total fat 12.4g; Sodium 236mg; Total Carbs 18.9g; Fiber 1.2g; Sugars 2.6g; Protein 4.9g

Crab & Tempura Shrimp Sushi Bake

Preparation Time: 15 minutes | Cooking Time: 4 minutes | Servings: 6

Ingredients:

5 cups cooked sushi rice
¼ cup seasoned rice vinegar
Non-stick baking spray
16 ounces imitation crabmeat, cut into small pieces
10 cooked tempura shrimp, cut up

½ cup mayonnaise
2 ounces cream cheese, softened
1 tablespoon Sriracha
3 tablespoons furikake

Preparation:

1. In a large-sized bowl, add the cooked rice and vinegar and blend to incorporate. Set aside to cool thoroughly. 2. For preheating: set your oven to broiler. 3. Grease a baking dish with baking spray. 4. For the crab mixture: in a bowl, add the crab, shrimp, mayonnaise, cream cheese and Sriracha and blend to incorporate thoroughly. 5. Place the rice into the prepared baking dish and with the back of a spoon, press downwards. 6. Sprinkle the top with furikake. 7. Place the crab mixture over the rice. 8. Broil for around 4 minutes. 9. Serve warm.

Per Serving: Calories 440; Total Fat 25.4g; Sodium 616mg; Total Carbs 47.9g; Fiber 2.5g; Sugars 3.1g; Protein 10.1g

Spinach & Mushroom Sushi Bake

Preparation Time: 15 minutes | Cooking Time: 32 minutes | Servings: 4

Ingredients:

Non-stick baking spray
2 cups cooked sushi rice
2 cups fresh mushrooms, sliced
2 cups fresh spinach, cut up
2 cloves garlic, finely cut up

2 tablespoons olive oil
Salt and ground black pepper, as desired
1 cup breadcrumbs
2 tablespoons nutritional yeast
2 tablespoons butter, melted

Preparation:

1. For preheating: set your oven at 375°F. 2. Lightly grease a baking dish with baking spray. 3. In a large-sized wok, heat olive oil over medium heat. Cook the mushrooms for around 5 minutes. 4. Add in the spinach, garlic, salt and pepper and cook for around 2 minutes. 5. In a large-sized bowl, add the cooked mushroom mixture and rice and blend to incorporate. 6. Place the mixture into the prepared baking dish and spread evenly. 7. In a small-sized bowl, add the breadcrumbs, nutritional yeast and butter and blend to incorporate. Spread the mixture in the baking dish. 8. Bake for around 20-25 minutes. 9. Serve warm

Per Serving: Calories 620; Total Fat 25.4g; Sodium 466mg; Total Carbs 70.9g; Fiber 6.5g; Sugars 5.4g; Protein 8.1g

Seafood Sushi Bake

Preparation Time: 15 minutes | Cooking Time: 15 minutes Serving: 6

Ingredients:

1 tablespoon rice vinegar
1 tablespoon white sugar
½ teaspoon salt
1 pound hot cooked white rice
Non-stick baking spray
2 (5-ounce) cans salmon, drained

2 (5-ounce) cans tuna, drained
6 ounces imitation crabmeat, cut up
6 ounces mayonnaise
4 ounces cream cheese, thawed
3 tablespoons scallions, cut up
2 tablespoons furikake

Preparation:

1. In a small-sized saucepan, add the vinegar, sugar and salt over medium-low heat and cook for around 2-3 minutes, stirring continuously. 2. In a large-sized bowl, add the cooked rice and vinegar mixture and blend to incorporate. Set aside to cool thoroughly. 3. For preheating: set your oven at 400°F. 4. Grease a baking dish with baking spray. 5. In a large-sized bowl, add the tuna, salmon, crabmeat, mayonnaise, cream cheese and scallions and blend to incorporate. 6. Place the rice into the prepared baking dish and with the back of a spoon, press downwards. 7. Sprinkle the top with furikake. 8. Place the seafood mixture on top. 9. Bake for around 10-15 minutes. 10. Serve warm.

Per Serving: Calories 515; Total Fat 30.4g; Sodium 946mg; Total Carbs 34.9g; Fiber 1.5g; Sugars 4.4g; Protein 30.1g

Mushroom Cream Cheese Sushi Bake

Preparation Time: 15 minutes | Cooking Time: 12 minutes | Servings: 6

Ingredients:

Non-stick baking spray
For the Rice:
⅓ cup unseasoned rice vinegar
3 tablespoons granulated sugar
For the Topping:
4-5 large oyster mushrooms, cut into slices
1 tablespoon soy sauce
½ teaspoon onion powder
½ teaspoon garlic powder
Salt and ground black pepper, as desired
2 teaspoons vegetable oil

1½ teaspoon salt
6-7 cups cooked sushi rice

¾ cup mayonnaise
2 teaspoons unseasoned rice vinegar
2 teaspoons agave syrup
¼ cup cream cheese
1-2 tablespoons Sriracha
Furikake, as desired

Preparation:

1. For the rice: in a small-sized microwave-safe bowl, add vinegar, sugar and salt and microwave for 60-90 seconds. 2. In a large-sized bowl, add rice and vinegar mixture and toss to incorporate. Set aside to cool. 3. For preheating: arrange a rack in top of oven. Set your oven to broiler. 4. Grease a baking dish with baking spray. 5. For the topping: in a bowl, add the mushrooms, soy sauce, onion powder, garlic powder, salt and pepper and blend to incorporate. 6. In a large-sized wok, heat oil over medium heat and cook the mushrooms for around 5-7 minutes. Remove from heat and set aside. 7. In a large-sized bowl, add the mayonnaise, vinegar and agave syrup and blend to incorporate. 8. Add the cream cheese and Sriracha and blend to incorporate. 9. Add the cooked mushrooms and blend to incorporate. 10. Place the rice into the prepared baking dish and with the back of a spoon, press downwards. 11. Sprinkle the top with furikake. 12. Spread the mushroom mixture on top of rice and sprinkle with a little furikake. 13. Broil for around 3-5 minutes. Serve warm.

Per Serving: Calories 630; Total Fat 22.4g; Sodium 546mg; Total Carbs 91.9g; Fiber 2.5g; Sugars 8.7g; Protein 8.9g

Tofu & Veggie Sushi Bake

Preparation Time: 15 minutes | Cooking Time: 23 minutes | Servings: 8

Ingredients:

For the Rice:
6 cups cooked sushi rice
¼ cup rice vinegar
For the Tofu Layer:
14 ounces extra-firm tofu, pressed, drained and thinly sliced
2 scallions, cut up
½ of nori sheet, finely sliced
For the Sauce:
1 cup mayonnaise
1 tablespoon Sriracha
1 tablespoon rice vinegar
1 teaspoon soy sauce
For the Greasing:
2-3 teaspoons sesame oil, toasted
For the Topping:
2-3 carrots, peeled and julienned

2 tablespoons sugar
1 teaspoon salt

4 tablespoons soy sauce
2 tablespoons sesame oil
2 teaspoons Sriracha

1½ teaspoons sugar
½ teaspoon garlic powder
½ teaspoon onion powder
¼ teaspoon ground turmeric

Preparation:

1. For the rice: in a small-sized microwave-safe bowl, add vinegar, sugar and salt and microwave for 60-90 seconds. 2. In a large-sized bowl, add rice and vinegar mixture and toss to incorporate. Set aside to cool. 3. For the tofu: in a large-sized bowl, add all ingredients and blend to incorporate thoroughly. 4. For the sauce: in a bowl, add all ingredients and whisk to incorporate. Refrigerate before using. 5. For preheating: set your oven at 375ºF. 6. Grease an 8x8-inch ceramic baking dish with sesame oil. 7. Spread half of the rice evenly in the baking dish and top with a thin layer of carrots. 8. Place the tofu mixture on top, followed by remaining carrots and rice. 9. Spread about ¼ cup of the sauce on top. 10. Bake for around 15-20 minutes. 11. Now set your oven to broiler and broil for around 2-3 minutes. 12. Serve warm.

Per Serving: Calories 410; Total Fat 7.4g; Sodium 646mg; Total Carbs 70.9g; Fiber 6.5g; Sugars 5.4g; Protein 10.1g

Cream Cheese Chicken Sushi Bake

Preparation Time: 15 minutes | Cooking Time: 15 minutes | Servings: 4

Ingredients:

Non-stick baking spray
¼ cup rice vinegar
2 tablespoons sugar
1 teaspoon salt
4 cups cooked sushi rice

1 pound cooked chicken, cut up
2 ounces cream cheese, softened
¾ cup light mayonnaise
¼ cup scallions, thinly sliced
1 nori sheet, crushed

Preparation:

1. For preheating: set your oven at 425ºF. 2. Grease a baking dish with baking spray. 3. For the sushi rice: in a large-sized bowl, add the vinegar, sugar and salt and whisk to incorporate. 4. Add in the rice and blend to incorporate. 5. In another bowl, add the chicken, cream cheese, mayonnaise and scallions and blend thoroughly. 6. Place the rice into the prepared baking dish and with the back of a spoon, press downwards. 7. Sprinkle the top with crushed nori. 8. Place the chicken mixture on top. 9. Bake for around 10-15 minutes. 10. Serve warm.

Per Serving: Calories 524; Total Fat 26.4g; Sodium 596mg; Total Carbs 49.9g; Fiber 5.6g; Sugars 5.6g; Protein 24.2g

---

Spam Sushi Bake

Preparation Time: 15 minutes | Cooking Time: 15 minutes | Servings: 8

Ingredients:

Non-stick baking spray
8 cooked spam slices
7½ cups cooked sushi rice
¼ cup sushi vinegar

1 nori sheet, crushed
1½ cups carrots, peeled and grated
1½ cups purple cabbage, shredded
1 tablespoon sesame seeds

Preparation:

1. For preheating: set your oven at 425ºF. 2. Grease an 8-inch baking dish with baking spray. 3. In a large bowl, add the rice and sushi vinegar and toss to incorporate. 4. In the bottom of baking dish, spread about 2 cups of rice and top with nori pieces. 5. Arrange the spam slices on top, followed by carrots and cabbage. 6. Sprinkle the top with sesame seeds. 7. Top with remaining rice. 8. Bake for around 10-15 minutes. 9. Serve warm.

Per Serving: Calories 360; Total Fat 8.4g; Sodium 466mg; Total Carbs 60.9g; Fiber 5.5g; Sugars 5.4g; Protein 8.1g

---

Salmon & Cream Cheese Sushi Bake

Preparation Time: 15 minutes | Cooking Time: 35 minutes | Servings: 6

Ingredients:

16 ounces salmon filet
2 tablespoons soy sauce, divided
Salt and ground black pepper, as desired
5 cups cooked sushi rice
⅓ cup rice vinegar
1 tablespoon sugar

4 ounces light cream cheese
3 scallions, cut up and divided
2 nori sheets, crumbled
1 tablespoon Sriracha
2 teaspoons sesame seeds

Preparation:

1. For preheating: set your oven at 400ºF. 2. Line a baking sheet with a piece of heavy-duty foil. 3. In a bowl, add the salmon filet, 1 tablespoon of soy sauce, salt and pepper and blend thoroughly. 4. Bake for around 20 minutes. 5. Meanwhile, in a large-sized bowl, add the vinegar, sugar and 1 teaspoon of salt and whisk to incorporate thoroughly. 6. Add the rice and blend thoroughly. 7. Remove the salmon from oven and flake it with a fork. 8. In a bowl, add flaked salmon, cream cheese and half of scallions and blend to incorporate. 9. Again, set your oven at 400ºF. 10. Place the rice into the prepared baking dish and with the back of a spoon, press downwards. 11. Sprinkle the top with nori pieces. 12. Place the salmon mixture on top evenly. 13. Drizzle the top with remaining soy sauce and Sriracha. 14. Sprinkle with sesame seeds and remaining scallion. 15. Bake for around 15 minutes. 16. Serve warm.

Per Serving: Calories 445; Total Fat 16.4g; Sodium 446mg; Total Carbs 56.9g; Fiber 3.5g; Sugars 4.1g; Protein 24.1g

Shrimp & Cream Cheese Sushi Bake

Preparation Time: 15 minutes | Cooking Time: 15 minutes | Servings: 8

Ingredients:

Non-stick baking spray
2 cups shrimp, peeled, deveined and cut up
4 ounces cream cheese, softened
¼ cup mayonnaise
3 tablespoons Sriracha

2 tablespoons soy sauce
1 teaspoon sesame oil
¼ teaspoon ground ginger
2 cups cooked sushi
2 tablespoons furikake

Preparation:

1. For preheating: set your oven at 400ºF. 2. Grease a baking dish with baking spray. 3. In a large-sized bowl, add the shrimp, cream cheese, mayonnaise, Sriracha, soy sauce, sesame oil and ground ginger and blend to incorporate. 4. Place the rice into the prepared baking dish and with the back of a spoon, press downwards. 5. Sprinkle the top with furikake. 6. Place the shrimp mixture on top of rice evenly. 7. Bake for around 15 minutes. 8. Serve warm.

Per Serving: Calories 544; Total Fat 23.4g; Sodium 896mg; Total Carbs 48.9g; Fiber 4.9g; Sugars 2.6g; Protein 24.2g

Crab & Avocado Sushi Bake

Preparation Time: 15 minutes | Cooking Time: 20 minutes | Servings: 8

Ingredients:

3 tablespoons rice vinegar
2 tablespoons sugar
1 teaspoon salt
4 cups cooked short-grain rice
Non-stick baking spray
8 ounces imitation crabmeat, cut up

¼ cup scallions, cut up
⅓ cup cream cheese, softened
⅓ cup mayonnaise
1 teaspoon Sriracha
¼ cup furikake, divided
1 ripe avocado, peeled, pitted and sliced

Preparation:

1. For the rice: in a microwave-safe bowl, add the vinegar, sugar and salt and the microwave for around 30-50 seconds. 2. In a large-sized bowl, add the cooked rice and vinegar mixture and blend to incorporate. Set aside to cool thoroughly. 3. For preheating: set your oven at 375ºF. 4. Lightly grease a medium-sized rectangular baking dish with baking spray. 5. In a large-sized bowl, add the crabmeat, scallions, cream cheese, mayonnaise and Sriracha and blend to incorporate. 6. Place the rice into the prepared baking dish and with the back of a spoon, press downwards. 7. Sprinkle the top with furikake. 8. Place the crab mixture on top evenly. Place the avocado slices on top.9. Bake for around 15-20 minutes. 10. Serve warm.

Per Serving: Calories 531; Total Fat 14.4g; Sodium 450mg; Total Carbs 84.9g; Fiber 1.5g; Sugars 6.4g; Protein 10.1g

Crab & Mushroom Sushi Bake

Preparation Time: 15 minutes | Cooking Time: 10 minutes | Servings: 12

Ingredients:

Non-stick baking spray
1 ounce dried shiitake mushrooms
cooking spray
1 (8-ounce) package imitation crabmeat, shredded
½ cup mayonnaise

½ cup sour cream
1 ounce flying fish roe
1 fish cake, cut into matchsticks
4 cups cooked short-grain rice
6 tablespoons furikake

Preparation:

1. For preheating: arrange an oven rack about 6-inch from the heating element. 2. Set your oven to broiler. 3. Lightly grease a 9x13-inch baking dish with baking spray. 4. In a bowl of hot water, soak the shiitake mushrooms for around 6-10 minutes. 5. Drain mushrooms and squeeze out excess moisture. 6. In a large-sized bowl, add the mushrooms, crabmeat, mayonnaise, sour cream, fish roe and fish cake and blend to incorporate. 7. Place the rice into the prepared baking dish and with the back of a spoon, press downwards. 8. Sprinkle the top with furikake. 9. Place the crab mixture on top evenly. 10. Broil for around 8-10 minutes. 11. Serve warm.

Per Serving: Calories 265; Total Fat 10.4g; Sodium 466mg; Total Carbs 35.9g; Fiber 2.1g; Sugars 4.4g; Protein 9.8g

Shrimp Sushi Cups

Preparation Time: 15 minutes | Cooking Time: 15 minutes | Servings: 6

Ingredients:

Non-stick baking spray
1½ cups warm cooked sushi rice
1 tablespoon plus 1 teaspoon seasoned rice vinegar, divided
3 nori sheets, quartered
⅓ cup mayonnaise
1 tablespoon Sriracha
1 tablespoon soy sauce

1-pound uncooked shrimp, peeled and deveined
⅓ cup seasoned panko breadcrumbs
1 tablespoon canola oil
2 tablespoons scallions, thinly sliced
½ tablespoon white sesame seeds, toasted
½ tablespoon black sesame seeds
½ avocado, peeled, pitted and finely cut up

Preparation:

1. For preheating: set your oven at 400ºF. 2. Lightly spray a muffin tin with baking spray. 3. Place the rice onto a rimmed baking sheet and spread rice in an even layer. 4. Drizzle the rice with 1 teaspoon of rice vinegar and toss to incorporate. 5. In a large-sized bowl, blend together the mayonnaise, Sriracha and remaining rice vinegar. 6. Reserve ¼ cup of the mayonnaise mixture into a small-sized bowl. 7. Add the shrimp and soy sauce into the remaining mayonnaise mixture and blend to incorporate. 8. Arrange a nori square into each prepared muffin cup. 9. Place about 2½ tablespoons of rice over each nori square and press into bottom of muffin cup. 10. Top each cup with 3 shrimp. 11. Bake for around 8 minutes. 12. Meanwhile, in a small-sized bowl, blend together the breadcrumbs and canola oil. 13. After 8 minutes of cooking, sprinkle each cup with breadcrumb mixture. 14. Bake for around 6-7 minutes. 15. Remove the muffin tin from oven and set aside to cool slightly. 16. Carefully remove sushi cups from muffin cups and transfer onto a serving platter. 17. Drizzle with reserved mayonnaise mixture. 18. Sprinkle with scallions and sesame seeds and serve.

Per Serving: Calories 294; Total fat 18.4g; Sodium 576mg; Total Carbs 19.9g; Fiber 2.6g; Sugars 13.6g; Protein 19.9g

Mixed Mushrooms Sushi Bake

Preparation Time: 15 minutes | Cooking Time: 30 minutes | Servings: 6

Ingredients:

Non-stick baking spray
For the Rice:
4 cups cooked sushi rice
3 tablespoons unseasoned rice vinegar
1½ tablespoons granulated sugar
For the Mushrooms:
1 tablespoon vegetable oil
1-pound fresh button mushrooms, thinly sliced
½ pound fresh shiitake mushrooms, thinly sliced
For the Sauce:
3 tablespoons mayonnaise

1½ teaspoons salt
2½ tablespoons Furikake

2 tablespoons soy sauce
1½ teaspoons chili paste
Salt, as desired

1 teaspoon Sriracha

Preparation:

1. For preheating: set your oven at 375ºF. 2. Grease a baking dish with baking spray. 3. For the rice: in a small-sized saucepan, add the vinegar, sugar and salt over medium-low heat and cook for around 2-3 minutes, stirring continuously. 4. In a large-sized bowl, add the cooked rice, Furikake and vinegar mixture and blend to incorporate. Set aside to cool thoroughly. 5. For the mushrooms: in a large-sized wok, heat the oil over medium- high heat. 6. Cook the mushrooms for around 4-5 minutes, stirring frequently. 7. Add in the soy sauce and cook for around 1-2 minutes. 8. Blend in the chili paste and salt and remove from heat. 9. Place the rice into the prepared baking dish and with the back of a spoon, press downwards. 10. Top with the mushroom mixture. 11. Bake for around 20 minutes. 12. For the sauce: in a small-sized bowl, add the mayonnaise and Sriracha and blend to incorporate. Set aside. 13. Serve warm with the drizzling of sauce.

Per Serving: Calories 470; Total Fat 28.8g; Sodium 260mg; Total Carbs 34.9g; Fiber 4.5g; Sugars 4.4g; Protein 24.1g

Crab & Mango Sushi Bake

Preparation Time: 20 minutes | Cooking Time: 20 minutes | Servings: 10

Ingredients:

For the Rice:

3 tablespoon rice vinegar

1 tablespoon white sugar

For the Furikake:

½ cup sesame seeds, toasted

½ cup roasted seaweed, crumbled

For the Crab Mixture:

7 ounces cream cheese, softened

¼ cup mayonnaise

1 tablespoon Sriracha

Salt, as desired

1 teaspoon salt

4 cups cooked rice

1 teaspoon salt

1 teaspoon white sugar

2 cups imitation crab, shredded

1 large ripe mango, peeled, pitted and cut up

1 medium cucumber, cut up

20 nori sheets

Preparation:

1. For preheating: set your oven at 390ºF. 2. For the rice: in a microwave-safe bowl, add the vinegar, sugar and salt and the microwave for around 30-50 seconds. 3. In a large-sized bowl, add the cooked rice and vinegar mixture and blend to incorporate. Set aside to cool thoroughly. 4. For the furikake: in a bowl, add all ingredients and toss to incorporate. 5. For the crab mixture: in a large-sized bowl, add the cream cheese, mayonnaise, Sriracha and salt and blend to incorporate. 6. Place the rice in the bottom of baking dish and sprinkle with a thin layer of furikake. 7. Place the crab mixture on top. Then spread the mango and cucumber on the crab mixture. 8. Bake for around 15-20 minutes. 9. Serve warm over nori sheets.

Per Serving: Calories 154; Total fat 8.4g; Sodium 414mg; Total Carbs 17.9g; Fiber 2.6g; Sugars 9.6g; Protein 4.1g

Tuna & Avocado Sushi Bake

Preparation Time: 15 minutes | Cooking Time: 10 minutes | Servings: 20

Ingredients:

For the Rice:

1-2 teaspoons sesame oil

4 cups hot cooked sushi rice

1 tablespoon rice vinegar

For the Tuna Mixture:

3 (5-ounce) cans canned tuna in oil, drained

4-5 tablespoon mayonnaise

For the Topping:

1 tablespoon nori sheet, crushed

1 teaspoon sesame seeds

4 avocados, peeled, pitted and sliced

2 teaspoons white granulated sugar

½ teaspoon salt

1 tablespoon Sriracha

¼ teaspoon salt

2-3 tablespoon Japanese mayonnaise

2-3 tablespoon Sriracha sauce

1 scallion finely cut up

Preparation:

1. For preheating: set your oven to broiler. 2. Grease a 9x9-inch baking dish with sesame oil. 3. For the rice: in a bowl, add all ingredients and blend to incorporate. 4. For the tuna mixture: in a bowl, add all ingredients and blend to incorporate. 5. Place the rice into the prepared baking dish and spread in an even layer6. Sprinkle the rice with crushed nori and sesame seeds. 7. Place the tuna mixture over rice and spread evenly. 8. Top with avocado slices and drizzle mayonnaise and Sriracha. 9. Broil for around 10 minutes. 10. Garnish with scallions and serve.

Per Serving: Calories 174; Total fat 2.4g; Sodium 176mg; Total Carbs 18.2g; Fiber 3.6g; Sugars 1.6g; Protein 8.1g

Tofu & Radish Sushi Bake

Preparation Time: 15 minutes | Cooking Time: 20 minutes | Servings: 4

Ingredients:

Non-stick baking spray
For the Tofu Mixture:
10 ounces tofu, pressed, drained and cut into thin strips
10 radishes, cut into small pieces
3 tablespoons light soy sauce
1 tablespoon rice wine vinegar
For the Rice:
4 cups hot cooked sushi rice
1 tablespoon rice wine vinegar

2 cloves garlic
1 teaspoon sugar
2 nori sheets, roughly cut up

½ tablespoon sugar
¼ tablespoon flaky salt

Preparation:

1. For the tofu mixture: in a bowl, add all ingredients and blend to incorporate thoroughly. Set aside for around 20-30 minutes. 2. For preheating: set your oven at 390ºF. Grease a baking dish with baking spray. 3. For the rice: in a large-sized bowl, add all ingredients and blend thoroughly. 4. Place the rice in the prepared baking dish and with the back of a spoon, press downwards. 5. Top with tofu mixture. 6. Bake for around 20 minutes. 7. Serve warm.

Per Serving: Calories 145; Total Fat 8.9g; Sodium 346mg; Total Carbs 15.9g; Fiber 2.8g; Sugars 1.9g; Protein 8.3g

Teriyaki Chicken Sushi Bake

Preparation Time: 15 minutes | Cooking Time: 20 minutes | Servings: 6

Ingredients:

2 chicken breasts, cut into thin strips
⅓ cup teriyaki sauce
2 scallions, cut up and divided
Non-stick baking spray
4 cups hot cooked rice
⅓ cup rice vinegar
2 tablespoons sugar

2 teaspoons salt
2 eggs, whisked
1 tablespoon canola oil
1 ounce dried shiitake mushrooms
Salt and ground black pepper, as desired
6 tablespoons furikake
3½ ounces quick melt cheese

Preparation:

1. In a bowl, add the chicken strips, teriyaki sauce and 1 scallion and blend to incorporate. Set aside to marinate for around 30 minutes. 2. For preheating: set your oven at 350ºF. 3. Grease a baking dish with baking spray. 4. For the rice: in a large-sized bowl, add rice, vinegar, sugar and salt and toss to incorporate. Set aside to cool. 5. Heat a greased wok over medium-low heat. 6. Add the eggs and spread into a thin circular layer. Cook for around 1 minute. 7. Carefully flip the egg and cook for around 20-30 seconds. 8. Transfer the cooked egg onto a cutting board and let it cool slightly. 9. Cut the egg into thin slices and set aside. 10. In a medium-sized wok, heat oi lover medium heat and cook the chicken strips for around 1-2 minutes. 11. Add in mushrooms, salt and pepper and cook for around 1 minute. 12. Remove from heat and set aside. 13. Place the rice into the prepared baking dish and with the back of a spoon, press downwards. 14. Top with chicken, followed by furikake, eggs, cheese and remaining scallion. 15. Bake for around 10-15 minutes. 16. Serve warm.

Per Serving: Calories 781; Total Fat 36.4g; Sodium 166mg; Total Carbs 86.9g; Fiber 7.5g; Sugars 9.7g; Protein 38.1g

Crab, Shrimp & Asparagus Sushi Bake

Preparation Time: 20 minutes | Cooking Time: 23 minutes | Servings: 6

Ingredients:

4 cups cooked sushi rice
¼ cup rice vinegar
1 tablespoon granulated sugar
1 teaspoon salt
Non-stick baking spray
1 tablespoon furikake
1 tablespoon sesame seeds, toasted
8 ounces crab meat finely cut up or shredded (or imitation crab

meat)
8 ounces shrimp cooked, finely cut up (or salmon, tuna, etc.)
½ cup cream cheese, softened
¼ cup mayonnaise
2 large Nori sheets, crushed
4 blanched asparagus stalks, cut into 1-inch pieces
2 tablespoons Sriracha mayo
2 tablespoons sushi sauce (of your choice)

Preparation:

1. In a small-sized saucepan, add the vinegar, sugar and salt over medium-low heat and cook for around 2-3 minutes, stirring continuously. 2. In a large-sized bowl, add the cooked rice, vinegar mixture, furikake and sesame seeds and blend to incorporate. Set aside to cool thoroughly. 3. For preheating: set your oven at 425°F. 4. Grease a 9×13-inch baking dish with baking spray. 5. In a small-sized bowl, add the crab, shrimp, cream cheese and mayonnaise and blend to incorporate. 6. Place the rice into the prepared baking dish and with the back of a spoon, press downwards. 7. Sprinkle the top with nori. 8. Place the crab mixture over the nori evenly and top with asparagus pieces. 9. Drizzle the top with Sriracha mayo and sushi sauce. 10. Bake for around 15-20 minutes. 11. Serve warm.

Per Serving: Calories 419; Total Fat 21.4g; Sodium 846mg; Total Carbs 46.9g; Fiber 4.5g; Sugars 4.9g; Protein 14.1g

Chickpeas Sushi Bake

Preparation Time: 15 minutes | Cooking Time: 10 minutes | Servings: 4

Ingredients:

Non-stick baking spray
For the Sushi Rice:
4 cups cooked sushi rice
2 tablespoons rice vinegar
For the Chickpeas Mixture:
3 cups canned chickpeas, drained
3 scallions, finely cut up
1 nori sheet, finely cut up
¼ cup mayonnaise
1½ tablespoons lemon juice

2 teaspoons sugar
1 teaspoon salt

1 tablespoon soy sauce
1 tablespoon hot sauce
½ teaspoon garlic powder
½ teaspoon onion powder
¼ teaspoon smoked salt

Preparation:

1. For preheating: set your oven at 350°F. 2. Grease a 9-inch baking dish with baking spray. 3. In a small-sized saucepan, add the vinegar, sugar and salt over medium-low heat and cook for around 2-3 minutes, stirring continuously. 4. In a large-sized bowl, add the cooked rice and vinegar mixture and blend to incorporate. Set aside to cool thoroughly. 5. For the chickpeas mixture: in a bowl, add the chickpeas and with a potato masher mash them. 6. Add the remaining ingredients and blend to incorporate thoroughly. 7. Place the rice in the bottom of baking dish and top with chickpeas mixture. 8. Bake for around 10 minutes. 9. Serve warm.

Per Serving: Calories 384; Total fat 17.4g; Sodium 1506mg; Total Carbs 50.9g; Fiber 11.6g; Sugars 10.2g; Protein 13.6g

Tofu Sushi Bake

Preparation Time: 15 minutes | Cooking Time: 13 minutes | Servings: 12

Ingredients:

For the Rice:
2½ cups cooked sushi rice

¼ cup rice vinegar

For the Tofu Mixture:
14 ounces baked tofu, grated
2 scallions, cut up
5 tablespoons mayonnaise

4 teaspoons lemon juice
1-1½ tablespoons Sriracha
½ teaspoons sea salt

For the Topping:
1 tablespoon mayonnaise
1 tablespoon Sriracha

½ teaspoons water
1 tablespoon sesame seeds

Preparation:

1. For preheating: set your oven at 400ºF. 2. Spray baking dish with baking spray. 3. In a bowl, add the sushi rice and vinegar and blend thoroughly. 4. For the tofu mixture: in a medium-sized bowl, add all ingredients and with a fork, mash to form a smooth mixture. 5. For the topping: in a small-sized bowl, add the mayonnaise, Sriracha and water and blend thoroughly. 6. Place the rice in the bottom of baking dish and top with tofu mixture evenly. Drizzle with the mayonnaise mixture. 7. Sprinkle the top with sesame seeds. 8. Bake for around 13 minutes. 9. Serve warm.

Per Serving: Calories 130; Total fat 7.4g; Sodium 246mg; Total Carbs 10.9g; Fiber 1.9g; Sugars 1.1g; Protein 5.2g

Salmon & Crab Sushi Bake

Preparation Time: 20 minutes | Cooking Time: 35 minutes | Servings: 10

Ingredients:

Salt and ground black pepper, as desired
8 ounce salmon filet
3 cups cooked sushi rice
2 tablespoons seasoned rice vinegar
1 tablespoon granulated sugar
¼ teaspoon salt

8 ounces imitation crab meat, cut up
3 ounces cream cheese, softened
⅓ cup mayonnaise
2 tablespoons Sriracha
1(17 ounce) package nori, crushed

Preparation:

1. For preheating: set your oven at 425ºF. 2. Line a baking sheet with parchment paper. 3. Rub the salmon fillet with salt and pepper. 4. Arrange the salmon onto the baking sheet. 5. Bake for around 18-20 minutes. 6. Remove the salmon from oven and set aside to cool. 7. Remove the skin of salmon fillet and with two forks, flake into bite-sized pieces. 8. Meanwhile, in a small-sized saucepan, add the vinegar, sugar and salt over medium-low heat and cook for around 2-3 minutes, stirring continuously. 9. In a large-sized bowl, add the cooked rice and vinegar mixture and blend to incorporate. Set aside to cool thoroughly. 10. Again, set your oven at 425ºF. Spray a 9-inch baking dish with baking spray. 11. In a bowl, add the salmon, crab, cream cheese, mayonnaise and Sriracha and blend to incorporate thoroughly. 12. Place the rice in the bottom of baking dish and sprinkle with crushed nori. 13. Place the salmon mixture on top. 14. Bake for around 12-15 minutes. 15. Serve warm.

Per Serving: Calories 214; Total fat 11.4g; Sodium 356mg; Total Carbs 22.9g; Fiber 1.6g; Sugars 2.6g; Protein 10.2g

Chapter 5 Sushi Salad Bowl Recipes

Jackfruit & Spinach Sushi Bowls

Preparation Time: 15 minutes | Cooking Time: 23 minutes | Servings: 2

Ingredients:

20 ounces canned unripe jackfruit in brine
Salt, as desired
1 teaspoon vegetable oil
1 cup cooked and seasoned sushi rice
1 tablespoon sesame seeds

¼ cup water
2 tablespoons teriyaki sauce
1 teaspoon olive oil
2 cups fresh spinach
1 nori sheet, toasted and cut into short strips

Preparation:

1. Drain the jackfruit and then rinse well. 2. Heat a non-stick saucepan over medium heat and stir fry the jackfruit for around 4 minutes. 3. Stir in water and ½ tablespoon of teriyaki sauce and cook, covered for around 15 minutes. 4. Uncover the pan and with 2 forks, shred the jackfruits completely. 5. Stir in remaining teriyaki sauce and salt and cook for around 1 minute. 6. In the meantime, in a non-stick frying pan, heat the olive oil over medium heat and cook the spinach for around 2-3 minutes. 7. Stir in the salt and remove from the heat. 8. Divide the rice into serving bowls, evenly and top each with jackfruit mixture, spinach and nori strips. 9. Sprinkle with sesame seeds and serve.

Per Serving: Calories 666; Total fat 7.2g; Sodium 1946mg; Total Carbs 24.8g; Fiber 3.4g; Sugars 5.6g; Protein 4.9g

Edamame & Veggie Sushi Salad

Preparation Time: 15 minutes | Servings: 4

Ingredients:

3 tablespoons soy sauce
2 tablespoons rice vinegar
1 teaspoon sesame oil
1 teaspoon agave nectar
1 cup frozen edamame
1 medium avocado, peeled, pitted and cut into bite-sized pieces

1 cup green cabbage, shredded
½ red bell pepper, seeded and cut up
2 carrots, peeled and shredded
¼ cup scallions, sliced
3 tablespoons fresh chives, finely cut up
3 cups cooked brown rice

Preparation:

1. In a small-sized bowl, add the soy sauce, rice vinegar, sesame oil and agave and whisk to incorporate. 2. In a large-sized salad bowl, add remaining ingredients except for rice and blend. 3. Divide the rice into serving bowls and top each with edamame mixture. 4. Drizzle with dressing and serve.

Per Serving: Calories 308; Total fat 8.4g; Sodium 446mg; Total Carbs 51.9g; Fiber 7.6g; Sugars 5.6g; Protein 10.2g

Salmon & Cauliflower Rice Sushi Salad

Preparation Time: 15 minutes | Servings: 2

Ingredients:

2 tablespoon sesame oil, toasted
2 teaspoon tamari
1 tablespoon rice vinegar
Salt, as desired
1½ cups frozen cauliflower rice, thawed

6 ounces cooked salmon, flaked
1 cup cucumber, cut up
½ of medium avocado, peeled, pitted and sliced
1 medium radish, thinly sliced

Preparation:

1. In a small-sized bowl, whisk together the sesame oil, tamari, vinegar and salt. Set aside. 2. Divide the cauliflower rice into serving bowls and top each with salmon, cucumber, avocado and radish. 3. Drizzle with dressing and enjoy.

Per Serving: Calories 374; Total fat 25.4g; Sodium 446mg; Total Carbs 9.9g; Fiber 4.6g; Sugars 3.6g; Protein 21.2g

Tofu & Edamame Sushi Salad

Preparation Time: 20 minutes | Cooking Time: 5 minutes | Servings: 4

Ingredients:

2 tablespoons rice vinegar
1 tablespoon sugar
½ teaspoon salt
3 cups hot cooked sushi rice
8 ounces firm tofu, pressed, drained and cubed
2 tablespoons corn starch
1-2 tablespoons sesame oil
2 teaspoons soy sauce
¾ cup mayonnaise

1 tablespoon Sriracha
1 tablespoon fresh lime juice
1 pinch salt
1 teaspoon sesame seeds
1 avocado, peeled, pitted and sliced
1 cucumber, sliced
2 carrots, peeled and sliced
1¼ cups frozen edamame
1 nori sheet, crushed

Preparation:

1. In a small-sized bowl, whisk together the vinegar, sugar and salt. 2. In a large-sized bowl, add the cooked rice and vinegar mixture and toss to incorporate thoroughly. Set aside to cool. 3. Coat the tofu cubes with cornstarch evenly. 4. In a large-sized pan, heat the sesame oil over medium heat and cook the tofu for around 4 minutes. 5. Add 1 teaspoon of soy sauce and cook for around 1 minute. 6. Remove from heat and sprinkle with 1 teaspoon of sesame seeds. Set aside to cool. 7. In a small-sized bowl, add remaining soy sauce, mayonnaise, Sriracha, lime juice and salt and whisk to incorporate. 8. Divide the rice into serving bowls and top each with tofu cubes, carrots, cucumber, avocado, edamame and nori. 9. Drizzle with mayonnaise mixture and serve.

Per Serving: Calories 604; Total fat 34.4g; Sodium 836mg; Total Carbs 59.9g; Fiber 6.6g; Sugars 8.6g; Protein 16.2g

Chicken, Pineapple & Edamame Sushi Salad

Preparation Time: 20 minutes | Cooking Time: 18 minutes | Servings: 4

Ingredients:

For the Chicken:
½ cup soy sauce
¼ cup water
¼ cup light brown sugar
1 tablespoon rice vinegar
1 teaspoon garlic, grated
For the Rice:
4 cups hot cooked sushi rice
2 tablespoons unseasoned rice vinegar
For the Vinaigrette:
⅓ cup mayonnaise
2 tablespoons water
2 tablespoons rice vinegar
For the Salad:
1 cup cooked edamame
1 cup fresh pineapple, cut up
For the Topping:
2 scallions, sliced

1 teaspoon fresh ginger, grated
1 teaspoon sesame oil, toasted
2 teaspoons cornstarch
1 tablespoon olive oil
1-pound boneless chicken breasts, cut into 1-inch cubes

1 teaspoon granulated sugar
1 teaspoon salt

2 tablespoons lime juice
1 tablespoon Sriracha
1 teaspoon sesame oil, toasted

1 cucumber, thinly sliced
1 carrot, peeled and thinly sliced

1 tablespoon sesame seeds

Preparation:

1. For preheating: set your oven at 400ºF. 2. Line a rimmed baking sheet with a piece of heavy-duty foil. 3. For the chicken: in a small-sized saucepan, add all ingredients except for oil and chicken and whisk to incorporate. Place the pan of sauce over medium heat and cook for around 2-3 minutes, whisking continuously. Remove from the heat and place half of sauce into a bowl. Add in the olive oil and whisk to incorporate. Set the sauce aside to cool slightly. 4. Reserve the remaining sauce for later use. 5. Add the chicken cubes and blend thoroughly. 6. Arrange the chicken cubes onto the baking sheet. 7. Bake for around 10-15 minutes. 8. Meanwhile, for the rice: in a large bowl, add all ingredients and toss to incorporate. Set aside to cool. 9. Remove the baking sheet from oven. 10. Immediately set your oven to broiler. 11. Coat the chicken cubes with the remaining sauce. 12. Broil the chicken for around 2-3 minutes. 13. Remove from the oven and set aside to cool slightly. 14. For the vinaigrette: in a small-sized bowl, add all ingredients and whisk to incorporate. 15. Divide the rice into serving bowls and top each with chicken and salad ingredients. 16. Sprinkle each with scallion and sesame seeds. 17. Drizzle with the vinaigrette and serve.

Per Serving: Calories 639; Total Fat 30.4g; Sodium 1996mg; Total Carbs 49.9g; Fiber 4.9g; Sugars 16.4g; Protein 45.2g

Teriyaki Pork & Broccolini Sushi Salad

Preparation Time: 15 minutes | Cooking Time: 5 minutes | Servings: 4

Ingredients:

For the Pork:
½ cup teriyaki sauce
¼ cup mirin

1½ pounds pork fillets, trimmed and cut into 1½-inch slices
1 tablespoon peanut oil

For the Rice:
4 cups hot cooked sushi rice

1 tablespoon sushi vinegar

For the Broccolini:
1 tablespoon peanut oil
2 bunches broccolini, halved lengthwise

2 cloves garlic, finely cut up
1 tablespoon water

For the Salad:
6 radishes, thinly sliced
2 scallions, thinly sliced

1 cup frozen edamame, thawed

Preparation:

1. For the pork: in a large-sized bowl, add teriyaki sauce and mirin and blend to incorporate. 2. Place ¼ cup of sauce mixture into a small-sized bowl and reserve for salad. 3. Add the pork slices into the bowl of remaining sauce mixture and toss to incorporate. Cover the bowl and refrigerate for around 15 minutes. 4. Meanwhile, for the rice: in a large-sized bowl, add the rice and vingar and toss to incorporate. Set aside to cool. 5. For the broccolini: heat oil into a wok over high heat. Stir-fry the broccolini and garlic for around 1 minute. 6. Add in water and cook with the cover for around 1 minute. 7. Transfer the broccolini onto a plate. 8. For the pork: heat oil in the wok over high heat. 9. Stir-fry the pork slices for around 2-3 minutes. 10. Transfer the pork slices onto a plate. 11. Divide the rice into serving bowls and top each with pork slices, broccolini and salad ingredients. 12. Drizzle with reserved sauce mixture and serve.

Per Serving: Calories 405; Total Fat 13.4g; Sodium 566mg; Total Carbs 31.9g; Fiber 2.5g; Sugars 6.4g; Protein 39.1g

Seafood, Egg & Cucumber Sushi Salad

Preparation Time: 20 minutes | Cooking Time: 7 minutes | Servings: 2

Ingredients:

For the Rice:
¼ cups unseasoned rice vinegar
2½ tablespoons granulated sugar

1 teaspoon salt
2 cups cooked sushi rice

For the Cucumber:
1 cucumber, thinly sliced
Salt, as desired
1 tablespoon unseasoned rice vinegar

¼ teaspoons soy sauce
¼ teaspoons sesame oil, toasted
1 teaspoon granulated sugar

For the Egg:
1 large egg
Pinch of salt

½ teaspoons vegetable oil

For the Salad:
4 large shrimp, peeled and deveined
⅓ lb. sushi-grade salmon, cut into thin slices
⅓ lb. sushi-grade tuna, cut into thin slices
1 avocado, peeled, pitted and sliced

4 lemon slices
2 ounces salmon roe
1 nori sheet, toasted
1 teaspoon sesame seeds

Preparation:

1. For the rice: in a small-sized saucepan, add the vinegar, sugar and salt over medium heat and cook for around 2-3 minutes, stirring continuously. 2. In a large-sized bowl, add rice and vinegar mixture and toss to incorporate. Set aside to cool. 3. For the salad: in a strainer, add the cucumber and ¼ teaspoon of salt and toss to incorporate. Set aside for around 10 minutes. 4. In a medium-sized bowl, add the vinegar, soy sauce, sesame oil, sugar and a pinch of salt and whisk to incorporate. 5. Squeeze the cucumber to release any excess moisture. 6. Transfer the cucumber into the bowl with vinegar mixture and toss to incorporate. Refrigerate before serving. 7. For the egg: in a small-sized bowl, add the egg and salt and whisk thoroughly. 8. In a small-sized non-stick wok, heat oil over medium-low heat. 9. Add the egg and spread into a thin circular layer. Cook for around 1 minute. 10. Carefully flip the egg and cook for around 20-30 seconds. 11. Transfer the cooked egg onto a cutting board and let it cool slightly. 12. Cut the egg into thin slices and set aside. 13. In a medium-sized saucepan of boiling water, cook the shrimp for around 2-3 minutes. 14. With a slotted spoon, transfer the shrimp into an ice bath to cool. 15. Divide rice into serving bowls and top each with seafood, cucumber, avocado and egg. 16. Garnish with lemon slices, salmon roe, nori and sesame seeds and serve.

Per Serving: Calories 511; Total Fat 28.4g; Sodium 166mg; Total Carbs 27.9g; Fiber 8.5g; Sugars 4.4g; Protein 28.9g

Teriyaki Chicken Sushi Salad

Preparation Time: 20 minutes | Cooking Time: 10 minutes | Servings: 4

Ingredients:

For the Rice:
4 cups hot cooked brown rice
1 nori sheet, finely cut up
1 tablespoon seasoned rice vinegar

½ teaspoon sea salt
½ teaspoon garlic powder

For the Teriyaki Chicken:
1½ pounds boneless chicken breast, cut into 1-inch pieces

1 (15-ounce) bottle teriyaki sauce

For the Sriracha Mayo:
⅓ cup mayonnaise
1-2 tablespoons Sriracha

2 teaspoon seasoned rice vinegar

For the Sushi Bowl:
1 English cucumber, sliced
1 large avocado, peeled, pitted and cut up

2 nori sheets, cut into triangles

Preparation:

1. In a large-sized bowl, add all rice ingredients and toss to incorporate. Set aside to cool thoroughly. 2. Meanwhile, in a large-sized wok, add the chicken pieces and ½ cup of the teriyaki sauce over medium heat and cook for 8-10 minutes, stirring occasionally. 3. Drain off the liquid from the wok and transfer the chicken cubes into a bowl. 4. Add 1 cup of teriyaki sauce and blend thoroughly. Set aside to cool. 5. For the Sriracha mayo: in a small-sized bowl, whisk together all ingredients. 6. Divide the rice into serving bowls and top each with chicken, cucumber, avocado and nori triangles. 7. Drizzle with the mayonnaise mixture and serve.

Per Serving: Calories 504; Total fat 22.4g; Sodium 1686mg; Total Carbs 44.9g; Fiber 2.6g; Sugars 30.6g; Protein 31.2g

Steak & Pineapple Sushi Salad

Preparation Time: 15 minutes | Cooking Time: 10 minutes | Servings: 2

Ingredients:

For the Steak:
1 clove garlic, finely cut up
1 teaspoon fresh ginger, finely cut up
2 tablespoons soy sauce
1 tablespoon sesame oil
1 tablespoon vegetable oil

1 tablespoon brown sugar
2 teaspoons rice vinegar
1½ teaspoons Japanese seven spice
½ pound beef fillet steak

For the Pineapple:
4-6 canned pineapple rings, cut in half

2 tablespoons light brown sugar

For the Salad:
2 cups cooked brown rice
2 ounces mixed salad leaves, torn
½ of avocado, peeled, pitted and sliced

3 radishes, thinly sliced
½ of cucumber, cut into strips
¼ cup cooked edamame

For the Topping:
2 scallions, finely cut up

1 teaspoon sesame seeds

Preparation:

1. For the steak marinade: in a bowl, add all ingredients except for steak and whisk to incorporate. 2. In a large-sized bowl, add half of marinade and steak and blend thoroughly. 3. Reserve the remaining marinade into the refrigerator. 4. Set the steak at room temperature for around 1 hour. 5. Heat a non-stick griddle over high heat. 6. Cook the steak for around 3-4 minutes per side. 7. Remove from the pan and place the steak onto a cutting board to rest for around 10 minutes. 8. Meanwhile, sprinkle the pineapple slices with brown sugar from both sides. 9. Heat a non-stick griddle over medium heat. 10. Cook the pineapple slices for around 3-4 minutes, flipping once halfway through. 11. Remove from heat and set aside to cool slightly. Cut the steak into thin slices. 12. Divide the rice into serving bowls and top each with steak slices, pineapple and salad ingredients. 13. Sprinkle each with scallion and sesame seeds. 14. Drizzle with reserved marinade and serve.

Per Serving: Calories 780; Total Fat 43.4g; Sodium 1009mg; Total Carbs 70.9g; Fiber 9.5g; Sugars 39.4g; Protein 27.1g

Smoked Salmon Sushi Salad

Preparation Time: 15 minutes | Servings: 6

Ingredients:

For the Spicy Mayo:

½ cup mayonnaise

¼ cup Sriracha

2 teaspoons rice vinegar

½ teaspoon sesame oil

For the Rice:

6 cups hot cooked sushi rice

¼ cup rice vinegar

2 tablespoons white sugar

½ teaspoon salt

For the Bowl:

3 cups smoked salmon, cut up into bite-sized pieces

2 avocadoes, peeled, pitted and cut up

2 cucumbers, cut into strips or discs

1 nori sheet, cut up

Preparation:

1. For the spicy mayo: in a bowl, whisk together all ingredients. Refrigerate to chill before using. 2. For the rice: in a small-sized microwave-safe bowl, add vinegar, sugar and salt and microwave for 60-90 seconds. 3. In a large-sized bowl, add rice and vinegar mixture and toss to incorporate. Set aside to cool. 4. Divide the rice into serving bowls evenly and top each with remaining ingredients. 5. Drizzle with mayo mixture and serve.

Per Serving: Calories 312; Total fat 17g; Sodium 356mg; Total Carbs 36.8g; Fiber 5.5g; Sugars 8.6g; Protein 13.3g

Mushrooms & Edamame Sushi Salad

Preparation Time: 15 minutes | Cooking Time: 10 minutes | Servings: 5

Ingredients:

4 cups fresh mushrooms, sliced

4 tablespoons soy sauce, divided

½ teaspoons smoked paprika

3¾ cups cooked rice (chilled)

3 medium carrots, peeled and grated

2½ cups seedless cucumber, sliced

1½ cups cooked edamame

5 scallions, sliced

5 nori sheets, cut into strips

2½ teaspoons sesame seeds

Preparation:

1. Heat a large-sized wok over medium high heat. 2. Cook the mushrooms with 2 tablespoons of soy sauce and paprika for around 10 minutes, stirring occasionally. Remove from heat and set aside to cool. 3. Divide the rice into serving bowls and top with mushrooms, carrots, cucumber, edamame and scallions. 4. Sprinkle the top of each with nori pieces and sesame seeds. 5. Drizzle with remaining soy sauce and serve.

Per Serving: Calories 300; Total Fat 3.9g; Sodium 316mg; Total Carbs 59.9g; Fiber 2.5g; Sugars 7.2g; Protein 12.1g

Spicy Tuna Sushi and Cucumber Salad

Preparation Time: 15 minutes | Cooking Time: 5 minutes | Servings: 2

Ingredients:

1 (5-ounce) can oil-packed tuna, drained

2 tablespoons mayonnaise

1 tablespoon Sriracha

2 teaspoons soy sauce

½ teaspoons rice wine vinegar

½ teaspoons sesame oil, toasted

1 tablespoon avocado oil

1 cup cooked sushi rice, chilled

¼ cup scallions, cut up

1 small cucumber, sliced

Preparation:

1. In a large-sized bowl, add the tuna, mayonnaise, Sriracha, soy sauce, vinegar and sesame oil and gently blend to incorporate. Refrigerate before serving. 2. In a large-sized wok, heat avocado oil over medium-high heat and cook the rice for around 3-5 minutes. 3. Remove from heat and set aside to cool. 4. Divide the rice into serving bowls evenly and top each with tuna mixture, cucumber and scallion. 5. Serve immediately.

Per Serving: Calories 444; Total fat 17.4g; Sodium 916mg; Total Carbs 38.9g; Fiber 5.6g; Sugars 9.6g; Protein 36.3g

Tuna & Kale Sushi Salad

Preparation Time: 15 minutes | Servings: 4

Ingredients:

2 cups hot cooked brown rice
1 cup fresh kale, tough ribs removed and thinly sliced
2 tablespoons rice vinegar, divided
¼ teaspoon kosher salt
2½ tablespoons soy sauce
1 teaspoon sesame oil, toasted
½ teaspoon Sriracha chili sauce

½ teaspoon fresh ginger, grated
1-pound sushi-grade ahi tuna, cut into ¾-inch cubes
¾ cup cucumber, cubed
1 small avocado, peeled, pitted and cubed
1 scallion, thinly sliced
1½ tablespoons white sesame seeds, lightly toasted

Preparation:

1. In a bowl, add the rice, kale, 1 tablespoon of vinegar and salt and toss to incorporate. Set aside. 2. In another large-sized bowl, add the remaining vinegar, soy sauce, sesame oil, Sriracha and ginger and whisk to incorporate. 3. Add the tuna, cucumber, avocado and scallion and gently and toss to incorporate. 4. Divide the rice mixture into serving bowls and top each with tuna mixture. 5. Sprinkle with sesame seeds and serve immediately.

Per Serving: Calories 344; Total fat 10.4g; Sodium 536mg; Total Carbs 31.9g; Fiber 5.6g; Sugars 1.6g; Protein 33.4g

Crab & Cauliflower Rice Sushi salad

Preparation Time: 15 minutes | Servings: 4

Ingredients:

12 ounces frozen cauliflower rice, thawed
3 tablespoons rice vinegar, divided
Sea salt, as desired
¼ cup mayonnaise
1 tablespoon Sriracha
8 ounces imitation crab meat, cut up

1 large avocado, peeled, pitted and thinly sliced
1 English cucumber, sliced
1 cup carrots, peeled and shredded
1 tablespoon pickled sushi ginger
1 nori sheet, broken into small pieces

Preparation:

1. In a bowl, add the cauliflower rice, vinegar and salt and gently blend to incorporate. 2. In another bowl, whisk together the mayonnaise and Sriracha. 3. Divide the cauliflower rice into serving bowls and top each with remaining ingredients. 4. Drizzle with mayonnaise mixture and serve.

Per Serving: Calories 284; Total fat 20.4g; Sodium 716mg; Total Carbs 16.9g; Fiber 6.6g; Sugars 5.6g; Protein 15.2g

Teriyaki Shrimp Salad

Preparation Time: 15 minutes | Cooking Time: 7 minutes | Servings: 4

Ingredients:

4 cups cooked rice
2 tablespoons rice vinegar
4 tablespoons light mayonnaise
1 tablespoon Sriracha
1 tablespoon water
2 teaspoons olive oil

1-pound large shrimp, peeled and deveined
3 garlic cloves, finely cut up
⅓ cup teriyaki sauce
1 English cucumber, cut up
2 small avocadoes, peeled, pitted and thinly sliced
1 tablespoon sesame seeds

Preparation:

1. In a large-sized bowl, add hot rice and vinegar and toss to incorporate. Set aside to cool. 2. In a small bowl, whisk together the mayonnaise, Sriracha and water. set aside. 3. In a wok, heat the oil over medium-high heat and cook the shrimp for around 3-4 minutes. 4. Blend in the garlic and sauté for around 1 minute. 5. Add the teriyaki sauce and cook for around 1-2 minutes. 6. Remove from the heat and set aside to cool. 7. Divide the rice into serving bowls and top each with shrimp, cucumber and avocado. 8. Drizzle with mayonnaise mixture and sprinkle with sesame seeds. 9. Serve immediately.

Per Serving: Calories 504; Total fat 16.4g; Sodium 816mg; Total Carbs 68.9g; Fiber 4.6g; Sugars 6.2g; Protein 23.7g

Shrimp Sushi Salad

Preparation Time: 15 minutes | Servings: 4

Ingredients:

For the Rice:
2 cups cooked brown rice
1 teaspoon rice vinegar

1 teaspoon soy sauce

For the Shrimp:
1 pound cooked shrimp
3 tablespoons mayonnaise
2 teaspoon Sriracha

1 teaspoon rice vinegar
1 teaspoon soy sauce

For the Bowl:
1 cucumber, cut up
1 cup carrots, peeled and grated

1 cup edamame, shelled
1 avocado, peeled, pitted and thinly sliced

Preparation:

1. For the rice: in a bowl, add all ingredients and toss to incorporate. 2. For the shrimp: in another large-sized bowl, add all ingredients and toss to incorporate. 3. Divide the rice into serving bowls and top each with shrimp, cucumber, carrot, edamame and avocado. 4. Serve immediately.

Per Serving: Calories 440; Total fat 15.4g; Sodium 576mg; Total Carbs 14.9g; Fiber 11.6g; Sugars 4.9g; Protein 39.5g

---

Crab & Avocado Sushi Salad

Preparation Time: 15 minutes | Servings: 4

Ingredients:

¼ cup mayonnaise
1 teaspoon soy sauce
1 teaspoon Sriracha
¼ teaspoons sesame oil, toasted
2 cup cooked sushi rice

8 ounces crab meat, cut into small pieces
½ of English cucumber, sliced
1 avocado, peeled, pitted and cut up
1 ounce nori sheets, cut into small pieces

Preparation:

1. In a medium-sized bowl, whisk together the mayonnaise, soy sauce, Sriracha and sesame oil. Refrigerate before using. 2. Divide the rice into serving bowls and top each with crabmeat, cucumber, avocado and nori pieces. 3. Drizzle with mayonnaise mixture and serve.

Per Serving: Calories 320; Total fat 20.4g; Sodium 690mg; Total Carbs 26.9g; Fiber 4.6g; Sugars 1.3g; Protein 15.1g

---

Seafood Sushi Salad

Preparation Time: 15 minutes | Servings: 4

Ingredients:

2 tablespoons rice vinegar
2 teaspoons sesame oil, toasted
1 teaspoon white sugar
Salt, as desired
1 cup cucumber, thinly sliced
¼ cup mayonnaise
2 tablespoons Sriracha

2 cups cooked and seasoned sushi rice
1 pound sashimi grade seafood (salmon, tuna, cooked shrimp, imitation crab)
1 avocado, peeled, pitted and sliced
¼ cup scallions, sliced
2 nori sheets, cut into strips
2 teaspoons sesame seeds

Preparation:

1. In a small-sized bowl, add the vinegar, sesame oil, sugar and salt and whisk to incorporate. 2. Add in the cucumbers and toss to incorporate. 3. In another small-sized bowl, add the mayonnaise and Sriracha and whisk to incorporate. 4. Divide the rice into serving bowls. 5. Top each bowl with seafood, followed by and avocado, scallions, nori sheets and cucumber. 6. Drizzle each bowl with mayonnaise mixture. 7. Enjoy immediately with the garnishing of sesame seeds.

Per Serving: Calories 589; Total fat 20.4g; Sodium 349mg; Total Carbs 71.9g; Fiber 9.6g; Sugars 3.1g; Protein 35.8g

Mango & Edamame Sushi Salad

Preparation Time: 15 minutes | Servings: 3

Ingredients:

For the Dressing:
2 tablespoons lime juice
2 tablespoons soy sauce
2 teaspoons sesame oil, toasted

2 teaspoons agave syrup
1 teaspoon garlic powder
1 teaspoon onion powder

For the Salad:
3 cups cooked brown rice
1 mango, peeled, pitted and cut up
1 avocado, peeled, pitted and cut up
1½ cups cooked edamame

1 cup red cabbage, shredded
¼ of cucumber, cut up
½ of small red onion, finely cut up
½ cup wakame seaweed salad

Preparation:

1. For the dressing: add all the ingredients into a small-sized bowl and whisk to incorporate. 2. Divide the rice into serving bowls and top with remaining ingredients. 3. Drizzle with dressing and serve.

Per Serving: Calories 590; Total Fat 17.4g; Sodium 666mg; Total Carbs 89.9g; Fiber 9.5g; Sugars 16.4g; Protein 18.1g

Tuna & Watermelon Sushi Salad

Preparation Time: 15 minutes | Servings: 4

Ingredients:

For the Rice:
4 cups cooked sushi rice
⅓ cup unseasoned rice vinegar

2 tablespoons granulated sugar
2 teaspoons kosher salt

For the Spicy Mayo:
¼ cup mayonnaise
1 tablespoon Sriracha

Kosher salt, as desired

For the Bowls:
12 ounces sushi-grade tuna
2 Persian cucumbers, thinly sliced
2 ripe avocados, peeled, pitted, thinly sliced

2 small watermelons, peeled, seeded and cut up
1 nori sheet, crumbled
2 teaspoons soy sauce

Preparation:

1. For the rice: in a small-sized microwave-safe bowl, add vinegar, sugar and salt and microwave for 60-90 seconds. 2. In a large-sized bowl, add rice and vinegar mixture and toss to incorporate. Set aside to cool. 3. For the spicy mayo: in a bowl, whisk together all ingredients. 4. Divide the rice into serving bowls evenly and top each with remaining ingredients. 5. Drizzle with mayo mixture and serve.

Per Serving: Calories 654; Total fat 39.4g; Sodium 456mg; Total Carbs 70.9g; Fiber 7.6g; Sugars 8.6g; Protein 26.1g

Teriyaki Spam Sushi Salad

Preparation Time: 15 minutes | Cooking Time: 5 minutes | Servings: 4

Ingredients:

1 (12-ounce) can teriyaki spam, cubed
2 tablespoons rice vinegar
1 tablespoon lime juice
1 tablespoon lite soy sauce
1 tablespoon sesame oil
4 cups cooked sushi rice

1 cup cooked edamame
1 avocado, peeled, pitted and cut up
½ cup carrots, peeled and shredded
¼ cup pickled ginger
4 scallions, thinly sliced
1 tablespoon sesame seeds

Preparation:

1. For the spam: heat a non-stick wok over medium heat. 2. Cook the spam cubes for around 3-5 minutes, flipping frequently. 3. Remove from heat and transfer the span onto a plate. Set aside to cool slightly. 4. For the sauce: in a small-sized bowl, add the vinegar, lime juice, soy sauce and sesame oil and whisk to incorporate. 5. Divide the rice into serving bowls evenly and top each with spam and remaining ingredients. 6. Drizzle with sauce and serve.

Per Serving: Calories 358; Total Fat 34.4g; Sodium 561mg; Total Carbs 43.9g; Fiber 7.5g; Sugars 5.4g; Protein 14.1g

Tuna & Edamame Sushi Salad

Preparation Time: 15 minutes | Servings: 2

Ingredients:

For the Salad:
2 cups cooked rice
2 (5-ounce) cans tuna, drained and flaked
1 avocado, peeled, pitted and sliced
For the Topping:
1 teaspoon pickled ginger
1 teaspoon wasabi
1 tablespoon soy sauce

1 cucumber, sliced
1 cup frozen edamame, thawed
1 tablespoon pickled carrots

1 tablespoon mayonnaise
1 teaspoon Japanese spice seasoning
1 teaspoon Japanese rice seasoning

Preparation:

1. For the salad: divide the rice into serving bowls and top each with remaining ingredients. 2. Serve with the garnishing of topping ingredients.

Per Serving: Calories 510; Total Fat 28.4g; Sodium 166mg; Total Carbs 38.9g; Fiber 8.5g; Sugars 4.4g; Protein 25.1g

Tofu & Avocado Sushi Salad

Preparation Time: 20 minutes | Cooking Time: 10 minutes | Servings: 6

Ingredients:

2 nori sheets, crumbled
6 ounces extra-firm tofu, pressed, drained and cut into ½-inch thick slices
3-4 tablespoons orange juice
1 tablespoon lemon juice
2 tablespoons brown sugar
2 tablespoons soy sauce

2 tablespoons rice vinegar
2 teaspoons orange zest, grated
½ teaspoon lemon zest, grated
4 cups cooked brown rice
1 avocado, peeled, pitted and thinly sliced
4 scallions, cut up
3 tablespoons sesame seeds, toasted

Preparation:

1. Heat a large-sized, non-stick wok over medium heat and cook the tofu for around 3-4 minutes per side. 2. Remove from heat and set aside to cool. 3. Cut the tofu into matchsticks. 4. For the dressing: add the orange juice, lemon juice and brown sugar into a small-sized saucepan over medium heat and bring to a gentle boil. 5. Cook for around 1-2 minutes. 6. Blend in soy sauce and vinegar and cook for around 1-2 minutes. 7. Remove from heat and blend in both zests. 8. In a large-sized bowl, add rice and ⅓ cup of dressing and toss to incorporate. 9. Divide rice into serving bowls and top with tofu, avocado slices and scallions. 10. Sprinkle each with nori pieces and sesame seeds. 11. Drizzle with remaining dressing and serve.

Per Serving: Calories 260; Total Fat 8.4g; Sodium 326mg; Total Carbs 40.9g; Fiber 5.5g; Sugars 4.4g; Protein 8.1g

Ground Beef Sushi Salad

Preparation Time: 15 minutes | Cooking Time: 12 minutes | Servings: 4

Ingredients:

For the Beef:
1-pound lean ground beef
1¼ cups scallions, finely cut up and divided
3 tablespoons soy sauce, divided
3 cloves garlic, finely cut up
2 tablespoons rice vinegar
For the Bowl:
4 cups cooked brown rice
1½ cups carrots, peeled and shredded

2 tablespoons honey
2 tablespoons fresh ginger, finely grated
¼ teaspoon red pepper flakes
1 tablespoon sesame oil

2 seedless cucumbers, thinly sliced

Preparation:

1. Heat a large-sized wok over medium-high heat and cook the beef for around 5 minutes. 2. Add ⅔ of the scallions and 1 tablespoon of soy sauce and cook for around 3-4 minutes. 3. Stir in the garlic and cook for around 1 minute. 4. In a small-sized bowl, whisk together the remaining soy sauce, vinegar, honey, ginger and red pepper flakes. 5. Add in the vinegar mixture and cook for around 2 minutes. 6. Remove from the heat and stir in the sesame oil. Set aside to cool. 7. Divide the rice into serving bowls evenly and spread the beef on top. Then top each with carrots, cucumbers and remaining scallion. 8. Serve immediately.

Per Serving: Calories 320; Total fat 22.4g; Sodium 456mg; Total Carbs 50.9g; Fiber 3.6g; Sugars 13.6g; Protein 25.6g

Seafood & Avocado Sushi Salad

Preparation Time: 15 minutes | Servings: 2

Ingredients:

2 cups cooked sushi brown rice
1 tablespoon plus 2 teaspoons rice vinegar, divided
1 teaspoon sugar
¼ teaspoon salt
1 cup cucumber, cut up
2 teaspoons sesame oil

2 teaspoons sesame seeds
8 ounces mixed seafood (tuna, smoked salmon, cooked shrimp and crabmeat)
½ of avocado, peeled, pitted and thinly sliced
1 nori sheet, cut into strips
1 tablespoon scallions, cut up

Preparation:

1. In a bowl, add the rice, 1 tablespoon of vinegar, sugar and salt and toss to incorporate. 2. In another bowl, add the cucumber, remaining vinegar, sesame oil and sesame seeds and toss to incorporate. 3. Divide the rice into serving bowls evenly and top each with seafood, cucumber mixture and avocado. 4. Sprinkle with scallions and nori pieces and serve.

Per Serving: Calories 490; Total Fat 13.5g; Sodium 346mg; Total Carbs 61.9g; Fiber 4.5g; Sugars 1.4g; Protein 33.3g

Crab & Carrot Sushi Salad

Preparation Time: 15 minutes | Servings: 5

Ingredients:

5 cups cooked sushi rice
6 tablespoons rice vinegar, divided
2 tablespoons granulated sugar
½ teaspoons salt
¼ cup light mayonnaise
1½ tablespoons Sriracha
¼ cup soy sauce

10 ounces lump crabmeat, cut into small pieces
1½ cups cucumber, cut up
¾ cup carrots, cut into matchsticks
1 large avocado, peeled, pitted and cut up
1 nori sheet, crumbled
1½ tablespoons pickled ginger, cut up
2 tablespoons sesame seeds

Preparation:

1. In a small-sized saucepan, add 4 tablespoons of vinegar, sugar and salt over medium heat and cook for around 2-3 minutes, stirring continuously. 2. In a large-sized bowl, add rice and vinegar mixture and toss to incorporate. Set aside to cool. 3. In a small-sized bowl, add the mayonnaise and Sriracha and whisk to incorporate. 4. In another small-sized bowl, add the soy sauce and remaining vinegar and whisk to incorporate. 5. Divide the rice into serving bowls and top each with crabmeat, cucumber, carrots, avocado, nori and pickled ginger. 6. Sprinkle the top with sesame seeds. 7. Drizzle with vinegar and mayo mixture and serve.

Per Serving: Calories 467; Total Fat 8.4g; Sodium 1166mg; Total Carbs 83.9g; Fiber 5.5g; Sugars 8.4g; Protein 12.1g

Tofu & Quinoa Sushi Salad

Preparation Time: 15 minutes | Cooking Time: 40 minutes | Servings: 4

Ingredients:

For The Tofu:
14 ounces extra-firm tofu, pressed, drained and cubed

For the Dressing:

½ cup tahini

¼ cup hot sauce

2 teaspoons lemon juice

1 clove garlic, cut up

1 teaspoon salt

For the Salad:

2 cups cooked quinoa

1 avocado, peeled, pitted and sliced

2 cups cooked edamame

1 cup purple cabbage, shredded

1 cup carrots, peeled and shredded

2 tablespoons furikake

Preparation:

1. For preheating: set your oven at 425ºF. 2. Line a baking sheet with parchment paper. 3. Arrange the tofu cubes onto the baking sheet. 4. Bake for around 40 minutes. 5. For the dressing: put all ingredients into a blender and process to form a smooth mixture. 6. Divide quinoa into serving bowls and top with tofu, avocado, edamame, cabbage and carrots. 7. Sprinkle each with furikake. 8. Drizzle with dressing and serve.

Per Serving: Calories 353; Total Fat 13.4g; Sodium 366mg; Total Carbs 45.9g; Fiber 0.5g; Sugars 3.4g; Protein 17.1g

---

Quinoa & Edamame Sushi Salad

Preparation Time: 15 minutes | Servings: 4

Ingredients:

For the Dressing:

¼ cup canola oil

2 tablespoons red wine vinegar

2 teaspoons white miso paste

¼ teaspoon sesame oil

½ teaspoon honey

½ teaspoon soy sauce

For the Salad:

2 cups cooked quinoa

½ cup cooked edamame

2 large carrots, peeled and shredded

½ small cucumber, sliced

½ avocado, peeled, pitted and sliced

For the Topping:

2 nori sheets, cut up

1 tablespoon sesame seeds

Preparation:

1. For the dressing: in a small-sized bowl, add all ingredients and whisk to incorporate. 2. For the salad: in a large-sized salad bowl, add all ingredients and blend to incorporate. 3. Place the dressing on top and toss to incorporate. 4. Sprinkle with nori pieces and sesame seeds and serve.

Per Serving: Calories 230; Total Fat 26.4g; Sodium 196mg; Total Carbs 65.9g; Fiber 11.5g; Sugars 3.4g; Protein 17.1g

Chicken & Cabbage Sushi Salad

Preparation Time: 15 minutes | Cooking Time: 10 minutes | Servings: 4

Ingredients:

For the Chicken:
2 tablespoons olive oil
21 ounces chicken thighs, cut into 2-inch strips
For the Sauce:
½ cup soy sauce
2 cloves garlic, crushed
2 tablespoons apple cider vinegar
2 tablespoons brown sugar
1 teaspoon sesame oil
1 tablespoon corn flour
For the Salad:
4 cups cooked sushi rice
1 cup cooked edamame
2 carrots, peeled and shredded
1 tablespoon sesame seeds
1 cup red cabbage, shredded
4 tablespoons mayonnaise

Preparation:

1. For the chicken: in a large-sized wok, heat oil over medium heat. 2. Cook the chicken strips for around 2-3 minutes per side. 3. Meanwhile, for the sauce: in a bowl, add all ingredients and whisk to incorporate. 4. Blend in ¾ of sauce and cook for around 3-4 minutes, stirring frequently. 5. Remove from the heat and set aside to cool slightly. 6. Divide the rice into serving bowls and top each with chicken, carrots, cabbage and edamame. 7. Sprinkle each with sesame seeds. 8. Drizzle with the remaining sauce and mayonnaise and serve.

Per Serving: Calories 565; Total Fat 26.4g; Sodium 1966mg; Total Carbs 40.9g; Fiber 6.1g; Sugars 10.4g; Protein 66.3g

Fish & Cucumber Sushi Salad

Preparation Time: 20 minutes | Servings: 4

Ingredients:

For the Rice:
3 cups hot cooked white rice
1 teaspoon sesame oil, toasted
1 tablespoon rice vinegar
½ teaspoon sea salt
For the Fish Mixture:
2 scallions, thinly sliced
1 tablespoon rice vinegar
½ cup soy sauce
¾ pound sushi grade salmon, cut into bite-sized cubes
2 tablespoons pickled ginger juice
¾ pound sushi grade ahi tuna, cut into bite-sized cubes
1 tablespoon sesame oil, toasted
For the Cucumber Salad:
¾ of cucumber, cut up
1 teaspoon sesame oil, toasted
2 tablespoons sugar
½ teaspoon sea salt
¼ cup rice vinegar
½ teaspoon red pepper flakes
For the Wasabi Sauce:
¼ cup mayonnaise
¾ teaspoon sesame oil, toasted
2 teaspoons wasabi paste
Pinch of sugar
2 teaspoons lemon juice

Preparation:

1. For the rice: in a large-sized bowl, add rice, vinegar, sesame oil and salt and toss to incorporate. Set aside to cool. 2. For the fish mixture: in another large-sized bowl, add the scallions, soy sauce, ginger juice, sesame oil and vinegar and whisk to incorporate. 3. Add the salmon and tuna cubes and toss to incorporate. Set aside. 4. For the cucumber salad: in a small-sized bowl, add all ingredients and toss to incorporate. 5. For the wasabi sauce: in a small-sized bowl, add all ingredients and whisk to incorporate. 6. Divide the rice into serving bowls evenly and top each with fish mixture and cucumber salad. 7. Drizzle with wasabi sauce and serve.

Per Serving: Calories 667; Total Fat 21.6g; Sodium 1174mg; Total Carbs 70.5g; Fiber 1.8g; Sugars 8.9g; Protein 46.3g

Chapter 6 Sushi Dipping Sauce Recipes

Sriracha Mayonnaise Sauce

Preparation Time: 5 minutes | Servings: 16

Ingredients:

1 cup mayonnaise
¼ cup Sriracha

½ tablespoon lemon juice
1 teaspoon ground black pepper

Preparation:

1. In a small-sized bowl, add all ingredients and whisk to form a smooth mixture. 2. Refrigerate before serving.

Per Serving: Calories 67; Total fat 5.5g; Sodium 140mg; Total Carbs 4.5g; Fiber 0g; Sugars 0.9g; Protein 0.1g

Onion Soy Ginger Sauce

Preparation Time: 10 minutes | Servings: 6

Ingredients:

¼ cup onion, cut up
1 tablespoon fresh ginger root, finely cut up
1 clove garlic, finely cut up
¼ cup soy sauce

1 tablespoon fresh lemon juice
¼ teaspoon white vinegar
¼ teaspoon white sugar

Preparation:

1. In a blender, add onion and remaining ingredients and process to form a smooth mixture. 2. Sauce is ready to serve.

Per Serving: Calories 13; Total fat 0g; sodium 640mg; Total Carbs 3.1g; Fiber 1.2g; Sugars 1.2g; Protein 1g

Easy Okonomiyaki Sauce

Preparation Time: 10 minutes | Servings: 16

Ingredients:

½ cup ketchup
7 tablespoons Worcestershire sauce

¼ cup oyster sauce
3 tablespoons sugar

Preparation:

1. In a small-sized bowl, add all ingredients and whisk to form a smooth mixture. 2. Refrigerate before serving.

Per Serving: Calories 23; Total fat 0g; Sodium 183mg; Total Carbs 5.6g; Fiber 0g; Sugars 5.3g; Protein 0.1g

Spicy Mayonnaise Sauce

Preparation Time: 5 minutes | Servings: 2

Ingredients:

2 tablespoons mayonnaise
1 tablespoon fresh lime juice

1 tablespoon chili-garlic sauce
½ teaspoon rice vinegar

Preparation:

1. In a medium-sized bowl, add all ingredients and whisk to form a smooth mixture. 2. Refrigerate before serving.

Per Serving: Calories 74; Total fat 4.9g; Sodium 105mg; Total Carbs 6.8g; Fiber 0g; Sugars 0.9g; Protein 0.1g

Homemade Tonkatsu Sauce

Preparation Time: 10 minutes | Servings: 8

Ingredients:

½ cup ketchup
2 tablespoons soy sauce
1 tablespoon brown sugar
1 tablespoon mirin

1½ teaspoons Worcestershire sauce
1 teaspoon fresh ginger, grated
1 clove garlic, finely cut up

Preparation:

1. In a medium-sized bowl, add all ingredients and whisk to form a smooth mixture. 2. Refrigerate before serving.

Per Serving: Calories 29; Total fat 0.1g; Sodium 447mg; Total Carbs 7g; Fiber 0.1g; Sugars 5.8g; Protein 0.6g

Flavorful Ponzu Sauce

Preparation Time: 10 minutes | Cooking Time: 5 minutes | Servings: 6

Ingredients:

¼ cup soy sauce
2 tablespoons mirin
2 teaspoons rice vinegar
¼ cup bonito flakes

1 (2-inch) piece kombu
1 teaspoon lemon zest, freshly grated
2 tablespoons lemon juice
2 tablespoons lime juice

Preparation:

1. In a small-sized saucepan, add the soy sauce, mirin, vinegar, bonito flakes, kombu and lemon zest over medium-low heat and bring to a boil. 2. Remove from heat and set aside to cool thoroughly. 3. Through a fine mesh sieve, strain the sauce mixture into a bowl. 4. Stir in lemon and lime juice. 5. Sauce is ready to serve.

Per Serving: Calories 41; Total fat 1g 4g; Sodium 611mg; Total Carbs 4g; Fiber 1g; Sugars 2g; Protein 2g

Miso Mayonnaise Sauce

Preparation Time: 10 minutes | Servings: 4

Ingredients:

¼ cup mayonnaise
1 tablespoon white miso

1 tablespoon fresh ginger, grated
2 cloves garlic, finely cut up

Preparation:

1. In a medium-sized bowl, add all ingredients and whisk to form a smooth mixture. 2. Refrigerate before serving.

Per Serving: Calories 74; Total fat 6.4g; Sodium 375mg; Total Carbs 6.9g; Fiber 0.6g; Sugars 1.6g; Protein 1.1g

Traditional Nikiri Sauce

Preparation Time: 10 minutes | Cooking Time: 5 minutes | Servings: 4

Ingredients:

10 tablespoons soy sauce
2 tablespoons dashi

1 tablespoon sake
1 tablespoon mirin

Preparation:

1. In a small-sized non-stick saucepan, add soy sauce, dashi, sake and mirin and whisk to incorporate thoroughly. 2. Place the pan over medium heat and bring to a gentle simmer, whisking continuously. 3. Remove the pan of sauce from heat and transfer into a bowl4. Set aside to cool thoroughly before serving.

Per Serving: Calories 40; Total fat 0g; Sodium 1921mg; Total Carbs 7.5g; Fiber 0.3g; Sugars .9g; Protein 2.5g

Delicious Dynamite Sauce

Preparation Time: 10 minutes | Servings: 2

Ingredients:

4 tablespoons chili sauce
2 tablespoons ketchup
2 tablespoons mayonnaise
1 teaspoon fresh lemon juice

1 teaspoon honey
½ teaspoon garlic powder
¼ teaspoon paprika

Preparation:

1. In a medium-sized bowl, add all ingredients and whisk to form a smooth mixture. 2. Refrigerate before serving.

Per Serving: Calories 85; Total fat 5g; Sodium 272mg; Total Carbs: 10.7g; Fiber 0.1g; Sugars 7.5g; Protein: 0.5g

Honey Wasabi Sauce

Preparation Time: 10 minutes | Cooking Time: 10 minutes | Servings: 4

Ingredients:

¼ cup honey
2 tablespoons wasabi paste

2 tablespoons soy sauce
1 tablespoon fresh lime juice

Preparation:

1. In a small-sized, non-stick saucepan, add honey, wasabi paste, soy sauce and lime juice and whisk to incorporate thoroughly. 2. Place the pan over medium heat and bring to a gentle simmer, stirring frequently. 3. Now adjust the heat to low and simmer for around 5 minutes, stirring frequently. 4. Remove the pan of sauce from heat and transfer into a bowl5. Set aside to cool thoroughly before serving.

Per Serving: Calories 93; Total fat 2.2g; Sodium 452mg; Total Carbs 19g; Fiber 0.3g; Sugars 17.5g; Protein 0.7g

Mustard Sauce

Preparation Time: 5 minutes | Serving: 1

Ingredients:

2 tablespoons soy sauce
2 tablespoons sake

1 tablespoon Dijon mustard
¼ teaspoon hot pepper sauce

Preparation:

1. In a small-sized bowl, add all ingredients and whisk to form a smooth mixture. 2. Serve immediately.

Per Serving: Calories 72; Total Fat 1g; Sodium 1066mg; Total Carbs 4.9g; Fiber 1g; Sugars 1.4g; Protein 4.6g

Mango Sauce

Preparation Time: 10 minutes | Cooking Time: 5 minutes | Servings: 12

Ingredients:

⅓ cup rice vinegar
⅓ cup granulated sugar
½ teaspoon salt

1 large ripe mango, peeled, pitted and cut into chunks
2 tablespoons vegetable oil

Preparation:

1. In a small-sized saucepan, add vinegar, sugar and salt and whisk to incorporate thoroughly. 2. Place the pan over medium heat and bring to a gentle simmer, whisking continuously. 3. Remove the pan of vinegar mixture from heat and set aside cool to thoroughly. 4. In a blender, add the vinegar mixture, mango and oil and pulse until smooth. 5. Transfer the blended sauce into a bowl and refrigerate to chill before serving.

Per Serving: Calories 62; Total fat 22.4g; Sodium 97mg; Total Carbs 9.8g; Fiber 0.5g; Sugars 9.4g; Protein 0.2g

Garlicky Sambal Oelek Aioli

Preparation Time: 10 minutes | Serving: 1

Ingredients:

3 cloves garlic, finely cut up
2 tablespoons mayonnaise
1 tablespoon sambal oelek

½ tablespoon white rice vinegar
Salt, as desired

Preparation:

1. In a small-sized bowl, add all ingredients and whisk to form a smooth mixture. 2. Serve immediately.

Per Serving: Calories 225; Total Fat 21.4g; Sodium 196mg; Total Carbs 8.9g; Fiber 0.5g; Sugars 0.4g; Protein 2.2g

Honey Mustard Mayo

Preparation Time: 10 minutes | Servings: 6

Ingredients:

½ cup mayonnaise
2 tablespoons honey
2 tablespoons prepared yellow mustard

1 tablespoon Dijon mustard
½ tablespoon lemon juice

Preparation:

1. In a medium-sized bowl, add all ingredients and whisk to form a smooth mixture. 2. Refrigerate overnight before serving.

Per Serving: Calories 165; Total Fat 15.9g; Sodium 235mg; Total Carbs 8.1g; Fiber 0g; Sugars 6.4g; Protein 0.3g

Homemade Yum Yum Sauce

Preparation Time: 10 minutes | Servings: 20

Ingredients:

1 tablespoon butter, melted
1 tablespoon mirin
1 cup mayonnaise
1 tablespoon ketchup
2 teaspoons rice vinegar
1 tablespoon granulated sugar

¾ teaspoon onion powder
¾ teaspoon garlic powder
¼ teaspoon paprika
⅛ teaspoon cayenne pepper
1-2 tablespoons water

Preparation:

1. In a medium-sized bowl, add all ingredients and whisk to form a smooth mixture. 2. Refrigerate before serving.

Per Serving: Calories 56; Fat: 4.5g; Sodium 103mg; Total Carbs: 4.1g; Fiber 0g; Sugar 1.8g; Protein: 0.2g

Sriracha Mayo

Preparation Time: 10 minutes | Servings: 4

Ingredients:

½ cup mayonnaise
2 tablespoons Sriracha

¼ teaspoon sesame oil, toasted

Preparation:

1. In a medium-sized bowl, add all ingredients and whisk to form a smooth mixture. 2. Serve immediately.

Per Serving: Calories 204; Total Fat 19.4g; Sodium 416mg; Total Carbs 13.2g; Fiber 0.5g; Sugars 3.1g; Protein 0.1g

Teriyaki Sauce

Preparation Time: 10 minutes | Cooking Time: 10 minutes | Servings: 12

Ingredients:

1 cup water
¼ cup soy sauce
1 tablespoon honey
5 teaspoons brown sugar

½ teaspoon ground ginger
¼ teaspoon garlic powder
2 tablespoons cornstarch
¼ cup cold water

Preparation:

1. In a medium-sized saucepan, add 1 cup of water, soy sauce, honey, brown sugar, ginger and garlic powder over medium heat and cook for around 1-2 minutes or until heated through, stirring continuously. 2. Meanwhile, in a small-sized bowl, dissolve cornstarch in ¼ cup of cold water. 3. In the pan, add the cornstarch mixture, stirring continuously. 4. Cook for around 5-7 minutes, stirring frequently.

Per Serving: Calories 18; Total fat 0g; Sodium 301mg; Total Carbs 4.4g; Fiber 0.1g; Sugars 2.8g; Protein 0.4g

Ginger Miso Sauce

Preparation Time: 10 minutes | Servings: 8

Ingredients:

¼ cup white miso paste
¼ cup water
2 tablespoons lime juice
1 tablespoon rice vinegar

2 teaspoons sesame oil, toasted
1 (1-inch) piece fresh ginger, finely grated
3 cloves garlic, finely grated

Preparation:

1. In a medium-sized bowl, add all ingredients and whisk to form a smooth mixture. 2. Serve immediately.

Per Serving: Calories 34; Total Fat 2.4g; Sodium 331mg; Total Carbs 5.3g; Fiber 1.5g; Sugars 1.4g; Protein 1.6g

Chinese Sweet Sauce

Preparation Time: 10 minutes | Cooking Time: 10 minutes | Servings: 4

Ingredients:

1 cup white sugar
1 cup chicken broth
2 tablespoons sesame oil
2 tablespoons white vinegar
1 teaspoon chile paste

¼ cup cornstarch
½ cup water
2 tablespoons dark soy sauce
1 clove garlic, finely cut up

Preparation:

1. In a small-sized saucepan, blend together the sugar and cornstarch. 2. Add in broth and remaining ingredients and blend to incorporate. 3. Place the pan of sauce over high heat and bring to a boil, stirring continuously. 4. Reduce the heat to low and simmer for around 5 minutes. 5. Transfer the sauce into a bowl and set aside to cool thoroughly before serving.

Per Serving: Calories 297; Total fat 7.4g; Sodium: 470mg; Total Carbs 58.4g; Fiber 0.1g; Sugar 51.6g; Protein 1.9g

Classic Aji Amarillo Sauce

Preparation Time: 10 minutes | Servings: 6

Ingredients:

1 small shallot, cut up
2 cloves garlic, cut up
2 tablespoons aji amarillo paste (yellow pepper paste)
½ cup mayonnaise
¼ cup Greek yogurt

¼ cup feta cheese, crumbled
1 tablespoon ketchup
2 tablespoons lime juice
Salt and ground black pepper, as desired

Preparation:

1. Put all ingredients into a high-powdered blender or food processor and process to form a smooth mixture. 2. Refrigerate before serving.

Per Serving: Calories 165; Total Fat 15.8g; Sodium 226mg; Total Carbs 4.9g; Fiber 0.5g; Sugars 2.4g; Protein 2.5g

Jalapeño & Cilantro Sauce

Preparation Time: 15 minutes | Servings: 6

Ingredients:

1 cup fresh cilantro leaves
3 jalapeño peppers, seeded and roughly cut up
2 scallions (green parts), cut up
2 cloves garlic, cut up
½ cup mayonnaise

¼ cup plain Greek yogurt
1 tablespoon lime juice
½ teaspoon salt
¼ teaspoon ground black pepper
2 tablespoons extra-virgin olive oil

Preparation:

1. Put all ingredients except for oil into a high-powdered blender or food processor and process to incorporate thoroughly. 2. While the motor is running, slowly add in oil and process to form a smooth mixture. 3. Refrigerate before serving.

Per Serving: Calories 182; Total Fat 19.6g; Sodium 326mg; Total Carbs 2.7g; Fiber 0.6g; Sugars 1.3g; Protein 1.3g

Sambal Oelek Aioli

Preparation Time: 10 minutes | Servings: 2

Ingredients:

¼ cup mayonnaise
1 tablespoon sambal oelek

2 teaspoons honey
½ teaspoon lime juice

Preparation:

1. In a medium-sized bowl, add all ingredients and whisk to form a smooth mixture. 2. Serve immediately.

Per Serving: Calories 224; Total Fat 23.8g; Sodium 216mg; Total Carbs 10.2g; Fiber 0.6g; Sugars 7.2g; Protein 1.1g

Sweet Orange Miso Sauce

Preparation Time: 10 minutes | Servings: 12

Ingredients:

¼ cup sweet white miso
¼ cup orange juice
¼ cup canola oil
1 tablespoon rice vinegar

1 teaspoon mirin
1 tablespoon fresh ginger, finely cut up
1 tablespoon orange zest, finely grated

Preparation:

1. In a medium-sized bowl, add all ingredients and whisk to form a smooth mixture. 2. Serve immediately.

Per Serving: Calories 58; Total Fat 5.4g; Sodium 141mg; Total Carbs 2.9g; Fiber 0g; Sugars 0.4g; Protein 0.1g

Simple Eel Sauce

Preparation Time: 5 minutes | Cooking Time: 5 minutes | Servings: 6

Ingredients:

½ cup soy sauce
½ cup mirin

½ cup white sugar

Preparation:

1. In a small-sized non-stick saucepan, add soy sauce, mirin and sugar over medium heat and cook for around 3-5 minutes, stirring frequently. 2. Transfer the sauce to a bowl and set aside to cool thoroughly before serving.

Per Serving: Calories 107; Total fat 0g; Sodium 1371mg; Total Carbs 27.6g; Fiber 0.2g; Sugars 22.4g; Protein 1.3g

Sweet Mayo Sauce

Preparation Time: 10 minutes | Servings: 8

Ingredients:

¼ cup ketchup
2 tablespoons pineapple juice
2 tablespoons white sugar

¼ cup mayonnaise
2 tablespoons white vinegar
1 tablespoon soy sauce

Preparation:

1. In a medium-sized bowl, add all ingredients and whisk to form a smooth mixture. 2. Refrigerate before serving.

Per Serving: Calories 51; Total Fat 2.5g; Sodium 96mg; Total Carbs 7.3g; Fiber 0.1g; Sugars 12.6g; Protein 0.3g

Conclusion

In closing, this sushi cookbook isn't just a compilation of recipes; it's a journey into the heart of sushi culture. From the simplicity of a classic maki roll to the intricate artistry of nigiri, each page holds a piece of Japan's rich culinary heritage. But beyond the ingredients and techniques lies a deeper story—the story of tradition, craftsmanship, and the joy of sharing food with loved ones. So as you embark on your sushi-making adventures with this cookbook in hand, remember to savor not only the flavors but also the essence of sushi itself—a timeless celebration of taste, craftsmanship, and community. Let these recipes be your guide, but don't be afraid to add your own twist. After all, the beauty of sushi lies not just in its perfection, but in its endless possibilities. Cheers to many delicious sushi-filled moments ahead!

Appendix 1 Measurement Conversion Chart

WEIGHT EQUIVALENTS

US STANDARD	METRIC (APPROXIMATE)
1 ounce	28 g
2 ounces	57 g
5 ounces	142 g
10 ounces	284 g
15 ounces	425 g
16 ounces (1 pound)	455 g
1.5pounds	680 g
2pounds	907 g

VOLUME EQUIVALENTS (LIQUID)

US STANDARD	US STANDARD (OUNCES)	METRIC (APPROXIMATE)
2 tablespoons	1 fl.oz	30 mL
¼ cup	2 fl.oz	60 mL
½ cup	4 fl.oz	120 mL
1 cup	8 fl.oz	240 mL
1½ cup	12 fl.oz	355 mL
2 cups or 1 pint	16 fl.oz	475 mL
4 cups or 1 quart	32 fl.oz	1 L
1 gallon	128 fl.oz	4 L

VOLUME EQUIVALENTS (DRY)

US STANDARD	METRIC (APPROXIMATE)
⅛ teaspoon	0.5 mL
¼ teaspoon	1 mL
½ teaspoon	2 mL
¾ teaspoon	4 mL
1 teaspoon	5 mL
1 tablespoon	15 mL
¼ cup	59 mL
½ cup	118 mL
¾ cup	177 mL
1 cup	235 mL
2 cups	475 mL
3 cups	700 mL
4 cups	1 L

TEMPERATURES EQUIVALENTS

FAHRENHEIT(F)	CELSIUS(C) (APPROXIMATE)
225 °F	107 °C
250 °F	120 °C
275 °F	135 °C
300 °F	150 °C
325 °F	160 °C
350 °F	180 °C
375 °F	190 °C
400 °F	205 °C
425 °F	220 °C
450 °F	235 °C
475 °F	245 °C
500 °F	260 °C

Appendix 2 Recipes Index

Made in the USA
Middletown, DE
16 December 2024

67352630R00061